# Changing Perspective Changing Life

Dr. Nivedita Ganguli

*Published by:*

**V&S PUBLISHERS**

F-2/16, Ansari road, Daryaganj, New Delhi-110002
23240026, 23240027 • *Fax:* 011-23240028
*Email:* info@vspublishers.com • *Website:* www.vspublishers.com

**Regional Office : Hyderabad**
5-1-707/1, Brij Bhawan (Beside Central Bank of India Lane)
Bank Street, Koti, Hyderabad - 500 095
040-24737290
*E-mail:* vspublishershyd@gmail.com

**Branch Office : Mumbai**
Godown # 34 at The Model Co-Operative Housing, Society Ltd.,
"Sahakar Niwas", Ground Floor, Next to Sobo Central, Mumbai - 400 034
022-23510736
*E-mail* vspublishersmum@gmail.com

Follow us on:

All books available at **www.vspublishers.com**

© Copyright: Author
ISBN 978-93-815882-8-4
**Edition 2015**

---

The Copyright of this book, as well as all matter contained herein (including illustrations) rests with the Publishers. No person shall copy the name of the book, its title design, matter and illustrations in any form and in any language, totally or partially or in any distorted form. Anybody doing so shall face legal action and will be responsible for damages.

*Printed at :* Param Offseters, Okhla, New Delhi-110020

# Acknowledgements

At the outset, I would like to thank the supernatural power above us for providing me with so many amusements in the form of unexpected experiences in life. I would also thank the same supernatural power for giving me a variety of experiences in life, which at that time, I thought as near death-experience, but after going through them and came out gracefully, became my learning experiences.

For me, the most visible supernatural power is my parents. So, I would like to thank my parents from the core of my heart, for giving me such beautiful seed of positive and valuable thoughts which has now grown into a plant with fruits that I am able to pass on to the people around. Besides my parents, my son Hemang has always been a strong source of support for me. Probably, I am in the journey of becoming a better psychologist after I got a beautiful gift in the form of my son, Hemang.

I would also like to thank my friends who have stood by me. Although the list of my friends is a bit long, let me mention some of the names: Vibha, Anita, Rekha, Usha and Gagan. I would also like to thank Mrs. Prem Lata Garg who has been very active and accommodating in giving me so much of exposure and guided me to a variety of learning experiences.

I would also like to thank all my participants from all parts of India for giving me many experiences through varied interactions. I wish to extend my heartfelt thanks to my online clients who have taken the pain to be in continuous developmental mode through 'online counselling'.

This book would not have taken this nice shape without V & S Publishers, for which I would like to thank Mr. Sahil Gupta for his tremendous faith in me as an author. My thanks also goes to my editor, Mr. Dibya and designer, Mr. Prosenjit for working with passion giving attractive touches to my expressions. I am sure, with the effort of each one of them this book is going to kindle a passion for life among readers.

# PREFACE

One day I was sitting silently and a bit upset and anxious over lot of personal and professional pressures. I thought of giving a break to my worries by changing my focus into something that I love to do. But at that difficult moment, it was difficult for me to remember what I love to do.

In moments of difficulty we tend to get tensed and become anxious. In a difficult situation, we too become difficult. The result is:

*Difficult situation + Difficult Person = Increased difficulty*

This exactly was my state also.

All of a sudden, my eyes fell on my laptop lying at the corner as if it was urging me to open it. The laptop seemed to be one of my most important friends. I started surfing – started skimming through famous quotes. One quote by Denis Waitley caught my attention. It said, "View life as a continuous learning experience." The quote kindled a spark in me. Immediately I queried myself, "What would this difficult situation teach me? What am I going to learn from such pressures?" And yes, my curiosity to learn from the situation increased. My anxiety vanished, as if I had been blessed with some magical power. It was like watching a movie and getting to know about its climax. The only difference was that as the movie was being made I wanted to create a 'happy ending'. And to create this happy ending, my focus shifted from 'anxiety' to 'handling'. It was a great experience. Within three days, I found that I could effectively manage everything around me. For me, life seemed manageable ever after.

The equation had changed for me now, as I understood the virtue of practising calmness in difficult situations. Finding solution to a situation with calmness became easy for me.

The equation changed to:

*Difficult situation + Calm person = Effective handling of the situation*

Thus, my journey of learning continued; I started searching for stories from my experiences, observations and interactions with various people.

It often happens that in the rush of our routine work, we miss out several important episodes in life. I have realised that the learning derived from each real life episode helps us deal with difficulties in a better way. Moreover, I have started seeing the events as if I am watching a movie intently, episode by episode, to find out what can

I pick up from these episodes and tried to analyse those episodes to unravel the best and useful learning for all my dear readers.

Along with beautiful fairy tales, we need to have real-life episodic learning which can bring about change in our life. This book would certainly give you a new dimension to think and discover the real beauty of life. Life presents us with many episodes which intend to guide us and impart valuable learning. But we generally ignore them. From now on, I am sure you would also look at each of these episodes critically and absorb its message, and bring about a significant change in your life and help others also to change their approach towards life.

Writing this book itself made me a different person. Now I am feeling more mature in handling relationships, stronger in facing challenges of life, and efficient in dealing with myself and others. I am sure this book would be a ready reckoner for you too.

I would love to know if these episodes have created any difference in your life. If it does, I shall be happy to receive your mail at: solveyourissues@gmail.com.

—Dr. Nivedita Ganguli

# CONTENTS

1. Power of service mentality --------- 9
2. Some amount of fog is good --------- 11
3. Something extra --------- 13
4. Fulfilling a last wish --------- 15
5. Throw ego down, or get drowned --------- 16
6. See the game clearly --------- 17
7. Train your mind --------- 18
8. Coming out of comfort zone --------- 19
9. Just bookish --------- 21
10. Use what is useful --------- 23
11. Magical power of appreciation --------- 25
12. Power of emotional brain --------- 26
13. Lost goal --------- 27
14. Proving Vs Improving --------- 28
15. Why did I think about Shoe? --------- 29
16. Showing Vs Being the best --------- 30
17. God's presence --------- 31
18. Today, Tomorrow and Day After Tomorrow --------- 32
19. Powerful impact of habit --------- 33
20. Mindset --------- 34
21. Pain is good --------- 35
22. End is important --------- 36
23. Where are you --------- 38
24. Hurdles --------- 39
25. Effect of comparison --------- 40
26. Mask --------- 41
27. Change the chair --------- 42
28. Conditional Vs Unconditional communication --------- 43
29. Being in tune with one self --------- 45
30. Power of similarity --------- 46
31. No END --------- 47
32. Real Present --------- 48
33. Put down your dark goggles --------- 49
34. Power of optionistic attitude --------- 50
35. Power of hope and damage of hope manipulation --------- 51
36. Thomas Edison also failed 1000 times --------- 53
37. Sympathy seeker Vs Cure seeker --------- 54
38. Effective Driving --------- 55
39. Feeling Vs Showing --------- 56
40. Patience Vs Tolerance --------- 57
41. Weakness Vs Way for improvement --------- 58

| | | |
|---|---|---|
| 42. | Similarity attracts | 59 |
| 43. | Principal with principles | 60 |
| 44. | Satisfaction dilemma | 62 |
| 45. | Laughing can be painful | 63 |
| 46. | Realistic optimism | 64 |
| 47. | Power of passionate work | 65 |
| 48. | Earning from learning | 66 |
| 49. | Magic of two ears | 67 |
| 50. | Mis-Take | 68 |
| 51. | Right spectacle | 69 |
| 52. | Magic of Enhancing of Self-Esteem | 70 |
| 53. | Not at the cost of mental peace | 71 |
| 54. | Judging and mis-judging | 73 |
| 55. | Fear – The worst enemy | 74 |
| 56. | Voices and Expressing Your Voice | 75 |
| 57. | Re-framing | 77 |
| 58. | Confidence Vs Over-confidence | 78 |
| 59. | Perfection is mere perception | 79 |
| 60. | Instruction not yet complete | 80 |
| 61. | Judgement – Are you empowered? | 81 |
| 62. | Intellectual EGO | 82 |
| 63. | Waiting for winning | 83 |
| 64. | Pattern of communication | 84 |
| 65. | Power of thought | 85 |
| 66. | SMS – Short Message Service or Shattered Mental Stability | 86 |
| 67. | Too much of everything is bad | 87 |
| 68. | Let them Get a Feel | 88 |
| 69. | Make over or take over | 89 |
| 70. | Service wins over knowledge | 90 |
| 71. | Change of focus | 92 |
| 72. | Active Vs Effective | 93 |
| 73. | Famous Vs Popular | 94 |
| 74. | Cut | 95 |
| 75. | Old is Gold | 96 |
| 76. | Power of self-control | 97 |
| 77. | Natural learning | 98 |
| 78. | Qualified but Unqualified to be Employed | 99 |
| 79. | Two people – One situation – Two responses | 100 |
| 80. | How actual is 'actually' | 101 |
| 81. | Reject better than react | 102 |
| 82. | Loss of mobile or loss of self-esteem | 103 |
| 83. | Competition Vs Envy | 104 |
| 84. | Discomfort leads to satisfaction | 105 |
| 85. | Stretching the knowledge zone | 106 |

# POWER OF SERVICE MENTALITY

A friend of mine, Gagan Kaushal everyday takes a rickshaw to reach her workplace. It had become a routine that she would have a tough time in giving direction to the rickshaw puller. She tried to explain the route each day by way of instruction to the rickshaw puller – "Take from the side of Ashoka Niketan road", and the rickshaw puller always used to take the rickshaw inside the Ashoka Niketan. "What the hell!" she used to think. Initially, she used to get angry on the rickshaw pullers internally but gradually the internal anger found expression by spilling it out. Her daughter Darika used to accompany her and witness this scene everyday. One day, Darika asked her mother, "Mamma, can I explain the route to the rickshaw puller?" Mamma said, "You can't. Can't you see how difficult it is for me!" Darika still requested. Mother finally yielded to the daughter's request. Taking the responsibility Darika said, "Uncle, take through the service lane of Ashoka Niketan." There was no confusion since then. They had peaceful journey thereafter.

### IN A NUTSHELL

1. Preconceived notion of 'I know it all' can block us from receiving wonderful experiences. Even children can gift us with lot of learning experiences.

2. Choosing the right words is the first level of right communication. If we don't, then the journey of misunderstanding starts and it would be a never-ending process.

   Right Communication ⟶ Enhanced Interpersonal Relation

3. In the above episode, there is mention of the word 'service lane'. If we focus on the word 'service lane', we can link it to our 'service mentality'. Service lane provides us with smooth walk; saves us from pressure of traffic. Similarly, service mentality saves us from pressure of work stress and gives us the magic of joyful living.

## FOOD FOR THOUGHT

*We will receive not what we ideally wish for, but what we justly earn. Our rewards will always be in exact proportion to our services.*

–Earl Nightingale

## SOME AMOUNT OF FOG IS GOOD

Delhi is famous for its fog in winters. It was 26 December '08. I was ready to go to office. As I opened the door, I was not able to take a single step forward. "Oh God! How can I go? It is so foggy!" a voice within me spoke. I was not able to see anything in front of me. But I had to go, as there was an urgent meeting. I have never experienced such a situation before and was being haunted by an unknown fear – "What will happen now?" I tried to gather courage from within and started the car. I was driving as slow as I could and tried motivating thoughts saying, "Many people are driving. If they can; I can also drive." I was aware that the situation is different compared to other days. So, I need to change my response also to meet the situation. I needed to drive very slowly which I was doing; I also switched on my parking lights and headlights. I took every possible step to cope with the difficult situation. I admit that I was attacked by fear off and on. But I was also forcing my determination to be a close friend at this juncture. I proceeded towards my destination beating the fear within me. I reached office exactly on time. I patted myself, "Yes, I did it."

I observed one more thing. As we were all driving very slowly with full caution, there was no accident.

### IN A NUTSHELL

1. Facing the fear eradicates the fear permanently. The courage gained from overcoming fear gets translated into other areas of life also.
2. Change may make us uncomfortable as we have a tendency to remain hooked to our zone of comfort. Stretching our comfort zone would help us to deal with the discomfort and enhance our confidence to face difficulties.
3. When we are focused on a single view, we are less prone to commit accidents (mistakes). So, little bit of fog is good to create focus on what we do.
4. Many a time when we become unconsciously competent (complete habitual pattern of working), we tend to be overconfident. So, moderate conscious competence can create peak performance.

## FOOD FOR THOUGHT

*It is not because things are difficult that we do not dare, it is because we do not dare that things are difficult.*

–Seneca

# SOMETHING EXTRA

It was 17 January '08. My brother's reception was on 18 January '08. So, all were busy in the last moment buying and final stitching of dresses. My mother who had just come from her native place was also in the same process. She wanted to wear an Assam silk sari which she had brought from Assam. But the problem was that just one day was left and the sari needed to be stitched. Would any tailor stitch at this eleventh hour? With doubt looming large in her mind, she went to all nearby tailors of the locality. But all of them pleaded helpless and excused. There were two reasons to it: first, it is difficult to stitch the sari so soon. Second, the 18 January '08 was a Sunday. On Sunday, shops are closed in Vadodara. I recalled one tailor who had stitched one of my suits long back. So, I took my sister along and went to him. After a formal talk, I said, "I have an urgent request..." I tried to give him an introduction... "You remember, long back I used to come for stitching of my suits. You know Mrs. Mitra.... my aunt?" He said, "Yes madam, you are Nivedita ma'am". It was great to know someone remembering your name whom you met long back. Then, I shared my request of stitching for my mother in urgency. I was honest in sharing that no other tailor is ready at this moment. He immediately said, "OK, this is Arati madam's?" (Arati is my mother's name). He knows my mother too. I thought, all the setting of background about me was useless. I shamefully said, "Yes." Then, he continued, "When do you need it?" I immediately started calculations verbally, "The function is in the afternoon. May be...." He interrupted, "Will it be OK if I give you at 11.00 a.m. tomorrow?" I was excited now, "Perfectly fine." But now my quiet sister intervened and asked, "But tomorrow is Sunday!" The tailor replied, "Don't worry. I shall come to the shop **just for you**."

Next day we were waiting for 11.00 a.m. thinking whether we would get the stitched material or not. It was 10.00 a.m. The phone rang. The person from other side said, "Madam, Arati madam's dress is ready. I wanted to remind you. Come as per your convenience."

There was a "vow" feeling within me. While writing this book, I thought to write the name of that tailor. But what was his name? I never bothered to ask! Hey... I need to develop this relationship skill which this tailor had taught me. Indeed there was 'something extra'.

## IN A NUTSHELL

1. Create 'vow' feeling in every interaction and turn every interaction into a 'Happy + Memorable Interaction'.
2. Keep going even if you face rejections. There is someone ahead waiting to help you.
3. Remembering someone's name gives a great feeling of joy to that person. Can we develop this skill?

## FOOD FOR THOUGHT

*Do not underestimate the determination of a quiet man.*
—Iain Duncan Smith

# FULFILLING A LAST WISH

After a lapse of 16 years, my mother visited Assam where she spent her childhood. When it was time to return and say "goodbye" to all, she gifted Rs. 100 to each of her brother's children. The car arrived and she sat in the car. Suddenly a thought flashed her mind and she shared it, "Oh! I am left with a last wish. All my other wishes are fulfilled." All of them asked, "What's that?" She said, "If I could have bought one cassette of Assamese music!" Her brother's son who was studying in class IX was standing nearby. He said, "Can you just wait for a while? I forgot one thing at home." They waited. The time of departure of her train was ticking in. Still no one wanted to hurt the feelings of that young boy. He returned in 10 minutes with two cassettes in hand. He said, "Aunt, take these cassettes. They have a variety of Assamese songs." His father asked, "Where did you get the money from?" He replied innocently, "Why? Just now Aunt gave us Rs. 100". It was a touching moment.

## IN A NUTSHELL

1. Think big. You can create a "permanent impact".
2. Identify the hidden wish of someone. Fulfill that wish. Then, realise the unlimited magic of joy flowing within your heart.

## FOOD FOR THOUGHT

*When we honestly ask ourselves which person in our lives means the most to us, we choose not the one who tendered us advice, solutions, or cures, but obviously the one who shared our pain and touched us with a warm and tender hand.*

–Henri Nouwen

## *Throw EGO down; or Get Drowned*

It was the time when I was leaving my office to reach the railway station in order to travel to Indore for a workshop. I was in a hurry. Oh! It was then I saw the narrow passage, which was both the exit and entry point getting crowded; I was also hearing a commotion as if some heated argument was going on over there. I found that a few people were trying to convince a girl who was shouting at the top of her voice. I was keen to know what was going on. I checked with the guard and he explained: "As soon as this girl was entering with her car, two vehicles were going out from here and the girl was asked to take her vehicle back so that the two vehicles can go out. Then it would be easier for her to enter. But she was adamant about getting in first despite the narrow space." She never listened to any elder or any colleague of her. It took almost one hour to manage the situation. It was after wasting everybody's energy and time she took the car back. All were staring at her. Though she was looking a bit embarrassed, a mask of overconfidence was seen on her face.

### IN A NUTSHELL

1. Many a time 'letting go' saves our valuable energy which we can invest in something which is more constructive.
2. It is important to know when to fight, when to ignore, when to talk and when to compromise. Life is a mix and match of these. The real flavour is created when we know when to use what to make of our own tasty life-recipe.

### FOOD FOR THOUGHT

Drugs, alcohol and ego. They are a bad mix.

–Don Dokken

## *See the game clearly*

There is a lot that we learn from children. Once, we (me and my son) were travelling by train. There was another family in the same compartment near our seat who were playing cards. My son moved to their right, then towards their left and then, he started climbing to the upper birth. I asked, "Where are you going?" He said, "I want to see the game." It was slightly annoying for me. I asked, "Why don't you sit here and see the game. Why do you need to climb up?" He replied calmly, "Mamma, I want to see the game clearly."

### IN A NUTSHELL

1. *We need to take ourselves out of the situation and select a position where we can look at other's position clearly and objectively.*
2. *If we have a holistic view of any situation, it will lead to a better decision.*

### FOOD FOR THOUGHT

*People believe I am what they see Me as, rather than what they do not see. But I am the Great Unseen, not what I cause Myself to be in any particular moment. In a sense, I am what I am not. It is from the Am-notness that I come, and to it I always return.*
— Neale Donald Walsch

## *TRAIN YOUR MIND*

My son is very fond of small children. One day he was talking to his cousin. It was a long conversation. I wished he hung up the phone which he was reluctant to do. I told him slowly, "If you talk so long, at the end of the month, mamma would be left with no money." This made him realise that it was time to end the conversation and say 'bye'. So, respecting my feelings, my son told his cousin, "Bye Namit." Namit instantly asked, "Are you going somewhere?" It was an unexpected question for my son. What made Namit guess that he was going somewhere! He replied, "No, I am not going anywhere, but what made you think so?" Namit responded, "Then why are you saying 'bye'?" For little Namit, the concept of 'bye' is associated with going somewhere.

### IN A NUTSHELL

1. *This is how our mind works. It works on how we train it. It works just as a child. Train your mind to expand its horizon and see broader picture.*
2. *Never assume. Once attacked with assumption, stop and ask, "What makes me think so?"*

### FOOD FOR THOUGHT

*Assumption is the mother of screw-up.*
— Angelo Donghia

## COMING OUT OF COMFORT ZONE

There are certain learnings associated with the memory of childhood. One such episode takes me back to the time when I used to ride a Scooty. I used to be very excited when I learnt to ride Scooty and was eager to show off my competence too. So I used to take either my mother or my sister for a ride. But once it was the turn of my grandmother. I was riding confidently until the moment my Scooty shook and my grandmother fell down with a loud scream. Oh God! She fell. My heart started thumping faster as I knew she had been hurt severely. I took her to the nearby hospital. She had two fractures and a few cuts here and there. I took care of her for 15 days when she was in the hospital. A sense of guilt was enveloping me off and on. As a result, I lost confidence even to touch the Scooty. The feeling of 'I can' turned into 'I can't'. To reach anywhere, I had to rely on some public transport which was not very convenient. A day came when I was not getting the service of public transport as there was some strike. I had to go for my tuition. Pondering over the options, my thought veered towards my Scooty. But fear started erupting again. There was a voice shouting within me, "Don't dare to commit the same mistake again. Miss the tuition, but don't touch the Scooty." The scene of grandmother's fall was agitating my mind. I forced myself to think about those moments when I rode confidently. I felt some confidence wellling up within and tried to wipe out the thought of accident and replaced it with positive thoughts of my successful rides in the Scooty. Then, I came back home and took a cloth to clean my Scooty. I wiped the dust; took my Scooty out. I just didn't know how my hands turned the Scooty towards the road smoothly and I reached my destination safely. 'I have done it' – a feeling resonated within me. Many years passed since that incident. And I reached a stage where I could think of buying a car. The first thought that came up was, "Can I?" The sentence did not end in only 'can I?' I gave several logical statements to myself to prove that 'I really can't.' The internal dialogues were like, "It is very difficult to drive in Delhi traffic. So many accidents occur on Delhi road (I was sure that it would be certain for me if I start driving). Can I really drive?" But the only episode that helped me was the successful recovery from my fear of riding my Scooty again. I thought, "I could do it when I was so young. Now I am more mature. If I could have done on that day, I can surely succeed today." And I did. I am a safe driver today.

## IN A NUTSHELL

1. Proceeding towards success till we fall is easy. But actual success comes when we can recover from a fall and proceed.
2. Create success memory at each step. You would certainly need those episodes when you grow up to help you navigate your way in tough times.

### FOOD FOR THOUGHT:

Move out of your comfort zone. You can only grow if you are willing to feel awkward and uncomfortable when you try something new.

—Brian Tracy

## Just Bookish

It was my workshop in one of the *Navratnas* with a topic "*Recreatiing Yourself.*" I challenged myself by telling the audience, "Today, I will not lecture on anything. You may ask questions and I will answer." The session progressed smoothy and I took so many questions such as 'We try to explain to our children what is good and what is bad. We encourage them but they are never encouraged. Why so?'; 'Someone misbehaved. I did not say anything. I just looked at him with stern eyes. Was it right?' I satisfactorily answered to all questions. But one person said, "Madam, in real life, all these are not possible to follow. Do you think these are practical? These are just bookish." I never expected such a harsh question. I had to accept the situation and devise a happy ending. I stimulated my entire thinking zone. I searched for the best possible answer and said, "Who wrote the books?" The participant answered, "Some person who had some idea or someone who thought he could write." I answered, "Absolutely, some idea or some thought based on his or someone else's experience. Isn't it?" The participant nodded. My courage to speak increased as I realised that I was moving in the right direction. I continued, "The author learnt something which probably took him a few years. But what an intelligent reader does? He picks up those experiences in just a few hours of reading and starts applying in life and creates a change in his or her life." The participant nodded again. I saw a book in front of the participant. It was something which helped me to validate my response. I asked, "Are you reading this book?" His response was affirmative. I asked, "Why do people read books? Why you being such a senior and experienced person reading a book?" He replied, "This is a good book and I have several things to learn from it." Great! I thought. He himself has the answer to his question. I was satisfied and so was he. I shared this experience with Shammi Sukh sir, who is a great author. He said, "Nivedita, I have one more point here. What came first? Doctors or books of medicine?" I replied confidently, "Doctors came first". He said, "Based on research, they write books which are then applied by the medical students. Then, they again proceed with some researches, and again the findings come out in form of books and the cycle goes on. Thus, the authors who write books have done many researches in their life and they bring up the findings in their books." This was a really great learning for me.

### IN A NUTSHELL

1. When you throw open challenge, be ready to face any difficulty with grace.
2. Be a book lover, learn, grow, and spread new thoughts to society.
3. Sharing of knowledge and experience doubles your wealth of knowledge and experience.

### FOOD FOR THOUGHT

*Of all the diversions of life, there is none so proper to fill up its empty spaces as the reading of useful and entertaining authors.*
—Joseph Addison

## Use what is Useful

Mr. Shammi Sukh is an author and the main motivator to my first book. One day, we were together at a workshop in a school. It was tea break. We, along with the participants went to the place where arrangements for tea were being made. I was enjoying my tea. Shammi sir was observing the surroundings minutely while having tea. He said, "Do you see something?" I said, "Yes, I can see all having tea." He smiled and said, "Yes, but are you seeing something else?" I said, "Yes, I am seeing the waiters serving tea, people are throwing the disposable glasses in the dustbin after finishing their tea." He said, "Yes, but what do you learn from this?" My mind was more focused on the session that I had to take after the tea break. I said, "Sir, please share your learning." He said, "See, when the cups are full they are picked up, and when they are empty, they are thrown away. Thus, when we are full with warmth and positive attitude, we are liked and appreciated by others. If we become empty of the positive traits, people would be away from us. We would be thrown away. Just as the cups were on demand till they were useful, similarly, we too need to learn to be useful."

### IN A NUTSHELL

1. *Everyday situations give us best learning experiences. Only awareness is required.*
2. *We always use the phrase, "What will be the use?" But we need to come out of this phrase and work on, "In which aspect of life can we use it?" If we ask the first question, we are keeping the option-door closed, but, if we are using the second question, we are keeping the option-door open. And we will be amazed to see that everything we learn can be put to use at an apporparite place.*
3. *When the whole world throws out something which they find useless, you pick it up and make it useful. Then the world buys the same treasure at a higher price. The cups were thrown away by the participants, but Shammi sir picked up a beautiful learning from the thrown out cups.*

### FOOD FOR THOUGHT

*Instead of looking at life as a narrowing funnel, we can see it as ever widening to choose the things we want to do, to take the wisdom we've learned and create something.*

–Liz Carpenter

# MAGICAL POWER OF APPRECIATION

n 17 January 2010, there was a dog show in Indirapuram, Ghaziabad. I went there with my son. We were excited to see many varieties of dogs standing with their proud masters who had taught them the skills. The dogs were displaying various tricks they had learnt. The masters, after showing a skill, were seen requesting the audience to give a heavy applause to motivate the dog for showing the next skill. This display of skills and request for applause went side by side. I found that the skills displayed were progressing from simple to diffi cult. The more it was diffi cult, the more applause they got. Moreover, what I also observed was that those dogs trained with motivation and appreciation displayed their talent with plenty of confi dence and dogs trained with stick sounded fearful. Their fear was showing up before the audience as they were nervous and seemed afraid that one mistake would bring them punishment. Because of nervousness, they were making more mistakes. But others, who were trained with love and motivation, made almost no error.

## IN A NUTSHELL

1. Even animals need positive motivation.
2. It is important that even the simplest thing should be praised. Then, the diffi cult skill becomes easier to execute.
3. In real life, we say, "This was so easy. Even a child can do it." But if an elder person is doing something which a child can do, is it not appreciable? Try playing outside under the sun for hours which a child can do. It would be really diffi cult.
4. Stick method can help someone to teach a skill, but in crisis, fear will takeover and ruin the quality of performance. Love and motivation is a powerful psychological medicine to develop internal security and confi dence. This will act like an emotional bulletproof jacket that can tackle any crisis one may face in life.

### FOOD FOR THOUGHT

Nine-tenths of education is encouragement.

–Anatole France

# POWER OF EMOTIONAL BRAIN

r. Sharma who had an injury in his hand was accompanied by Mrs. Neena when he came to the doctor. The doctor examined the hand of Mr. Sharma and confirmed that dead skin was coming out. The doctor said, "Can I remove this dead skin? This might create problem in case it rubs with your clothes." Mr. Sharma agreed. Then, the doctor took out a scissor to cut the dead skin. While cutting, both Mr. Sharma and Mrs. Neena, looked the other way. Although the skin was dead, it seemed to them the doctor was cutting Mr. Sharma's hand.

### IN A NUTSHELL

1. Although they knew that the skin was dead, they were not able to see it getting cut. But do we ever realise how every day we cut the emotions of people who are fully alive?
2. Although they know that cutting dead skin will not be painful, they were not able to see it getting cut. It is the effect of our emotional brain. Our logical brain knows that this would not be painful, but the emotional brain feels the pain. Thus, in the fast changing logical world, it is important to feel the emotional pain to bring about a change in society.

### FOOD FOR THOUGHT

Little deeds are like little seeds, they grow to flowers or to weeds.

–Daniel D. Palmer

# Lost Goal

ince childhood, we have been hearing words like, "Out of sight, out of mind." Many a time, it is useful but at times, it can be harmful too especially at a time the 'mall culture' is making all things too visible. That day, I went with one of my friends to a mall. She had taken a list with her and estimated that she would be requiring Rs. 2000 to buy all the listed items. At the end, to her surprise, she received a hefty bill of Rs. 5000/-. I asked her, "Where is your list?" She said, "It is in the purse." I said, "But you did not take out the list!" She replied, "It was not required as I was able to see everything I needed."

## IN A NUTSHELL

1. Since she was able to see everything, she felt 'she wanted everything'.
2. Our mind needs a certain control mechanism. Thus, the shopping list could be a tool of control for the mind when there was too many visible items to buy.
3. This applies to our goals too. We don't make a list of our priorities. So we get drowned in the river of 'visible doings'. For example, when we plan to write a book, the daily visible routine starts blocking our goal of writing and writing takes a backseat. So we should be aware of our goals and priorities and act accordingly.
4. It so happens that many a time, we start many things out of enthusiasm and then get lost in something else.

## FOOD FOR THOUGHT

*Our plans misfire because they have no aim. When a man does not know to which harbour he is sailing for, no wind is the right wind.*

–Seneca

## *Proving Vs Improving*

ne day I was talking to a person who had a clear aim about being successful. He said frequently, "I want to prove myself." But I found that his words were filled with anxiety. He used to say: "I don't know what she thinks about herself! She just got promotion with buttering. Actuallly, she is nothing"; "God is not favouring me. My luck is also not favoring me"; "I don't know why I fail in whatever I do!" He was sounding negative about himself, about his business, about his talent and also about others. It seemed he was developing an attitude of seeking sympathy from others. I realised that rather than proving himself he needs to improve himself. He needed to improve his thoughts and the words he was using for himself and others. When I gave this feedback, he was aggressive. But, after a few days, he understood what I said. We jointly worked for his improvement. Within two months, changes could be noticed in the way he used his language and his overall attitude to others. Results too turned positive for him.

### IN A NUTSHELL

1. *If we improve, we need not prove.*
2. *When we are weak, we struggle to prove ourselves. Once we develop the inner strength to improve, there is no need to prove. It becomes easy for others to see the result.*
3. *Make a choice: Prove and be anxious or Improve and grow. The word IMPROVED can be considered as "I am proved".*

### FOOD FOR THOUGHT

*Unless you try to do something beyond what you have mastered, you will never grow.*

–C.R. Lawton

## *Why did I think about Shoe?*

was conducting a workshop for a company. At the workshop, it was found that one of my shoes had pinched. I was worried whether the shoe in the other foot would also pinch. I was more concerned about my shoe than the workshop. I was worried as I had another workshop on the next day and there was little time to buy another pair of shoes. So the thought of a torn shoe started troubling my mind. I was thinking about the shoe sub-consciously and was trying consciously to focus on the workshop. During lunch, I got a call from one of my clients, who asked me, "Ma'am, what is the number of your shoe?" It was a real surprise for me. 'What? How did he know that I badly needed a pair of shoes?' I asked, "Why?" He said, "Ma'am you tell me. I shall give you the reason later." I was feeling embarrassed and did not want him to get me a pair of shoes. So I said, "I exactly don't know about the size as it differs from one company to another." He said "OK" and put the phone down. In the evening, when I reached home, my son said that someone had left a box for me. Yes, it was a box that had a pair of shoes inside. The next day, I conducted the workshop with the new pair of shoes. Isn't it amazing?

### IN A NUTSHELL

1. What we think intensely can turn into reality. So, mind your thoughts. I thought about the shoe intensely and got it; so, why not think about 'shoe business'? Think BIG and you will achieve it.
2. Feelings of joy got from giving are more important and enjoyable than when we get something. Thus, give not for the sake of name or fame but for the sake of contributing to feelings. Even small things can make a great difference in feelings. So start giving your time to the old and needy, you will really feel very contended and blessed.

### FOOD FOR THOUGHT

*To visualise is to see what is not there, what is not real – a dream. To visualise is, in fact, to make visual lies. Visual lies, however, have a way of coming true.*

–Peter McWilliams

## *Showing Vs Being the Best*

team from a newspaper came to an organisation in order to take feedback from a hundred employees for finalising some award. I happened to be there with the general manager. The team was very cordially received and seated comfortably. The group members called up the secretary to discuss about the department which could give a positive feedback. Then it was specifically mentioned not to get the feedback form filled up by the accounts department as they had some dissatisfied staff who had aired many grievances recently. Finally, it was decided to focus on one hundred 'good people' who would provide positive (even false) feedback. Despite the targeted selection it was found that even those best '100' did not give a positive feedback and it was poor feedback what they eventually got.

### IN A NUTSHELL

1. *When we try to 'show our best', our hidden fakeness would show up. But, when we are 'at our best', we would move towards excellence.*
2. *We all know our brand value. We know what we have delivered. Giving feedback to ourselves if not from others is more important.*

### FOOD FOR THOUGHT

*Telling lies and showing off to get attention are mistakes I made that I don't want my kids to make.*

–Jane Fonda

## GOD'S PRESENCE

o develop the 'power of introspection', I started training my son on writing letters to God every day. One day, he came to me with visible anxiety and asked, "Mamma, what if I cut after writing? Will God be able to see it?" I was not able to understand. I asked, "What do you mean?" He said, "See, if I have done three mistakes and I write about two, and then, further cut one more, will God be able to see two or three or just one?" I said that God would be able to see what was honest. He was convinced. But then, he said, "If God knows what is true then why does he want us to write it?" I was slightly confused. Still maintaining my balance, I said, "So that you can know how much honesty you have within. Moreover, you would feel closer to some supernatural power when you write to HIM."

### IN A NUTSHELL

1. This child had a feeling that there is a 'watchful eye' while he is doing something. If we try to project ourselves as good, there would be discrepancy between our real and ideal self which can create serious psychological problem.
2. Writing about oneself is an amazing exercise of 'introspection'. We all can grow spiritually if we start introspecting every day and plan modifying our errors.

### FOOD FOR THOUGHT

A man, who realises the potential of his mind by means of introspection and contemplation, will not be lacking in self-confidence. He has control over his mind and can realise its full potential.

–Sam Veda

## *Today, Tomorrow and Day After Tomorrow*

t was a Thursday morning. I was suffering from cold. Headache was also troubling me. Someone called me and wished me 'good morning' and asked "how are you?" I said, "I have ache in my head, cold in nose, laptop in front, and phone on ears." He smiled and said, "So, why don't you take some medicine?" I said, "It is perfectly fine. I am waiting for the Sunday so that I can sleep well." He said, "But ma'am, Sunday is far now. Today…, tomorrow… and day after tomorrow." I said, "How come so late? It's just today, tomorrow and day after tomorrow!" Our tones were clearly in contrast. His tone reflected as if Sunday is far away, and my tone reflected as if it is too near. He said, "Great! The way you said seems so positive."

### IN A NUTSHELL

1. What we say doesn't matter. How we say it makes great difference in relationship.
2. Physical state may not be in our hand but creating a 'feel good' factor is always in our hand. 'Feel good' factor would then lead to a physical wellbeing.
3. Today, tomorrow and day-after-tomorrow – these three words echoed in my ears for a long time. 'Tomorrow' has the word which puts things in row, day-after-tomorrow again has after in row. The word to-day has 'to and day'. This is the actual 'to-do' day. Thus, if we take care of our emotions and actions of the 'to-do' day', the lined up 'rows' (tomorrow) and 'after rows' (day after tomorrow) will automatically be in perfect order. The first person in a row has to be in the right place and then other people in the row would fall in right places.

### FOOD FOR THOUGHT

Once you replace negative thoughts with positive ones, you'll start having positive results.

—Willie Nelson

# POWERFUL IMPACT OF *HABIT*

r. Rituraj, whom I met in a workshop, was a senior manager (Training) in a reputed company. While coming back from the workshop, he shared a lot of anecdotes with me. One was about his trip to Allahabad. While driving there, one of his relatives was sitting next to his seat. After being seated, Mr. Rituraj was about to tie the seatbelt. His relative said, "What are you doing? It is not needed here." Mr. Rituraj said, "Oh! It is a habit now as in Delhi we have to tie the seatbelt." His relative was more concerned about his status. He said, "But everyone will look at you and take you to be a fool." Mr. Rituraj said, "It's O.K. Let them think. We don't have any control on what others think." His relative had no choice but to be quiet.

## IN A NUTSHELL

1. Habit is very powerful. Whether positive or negative, we always tend to resist or breaking it. Mr. Rituraj had a habit of tying seatbelt and when his relative questioned, he resisted. Inculcate powerful positive *HABITs*.
2. We do not die once. We die many times because of 'fear of judgment'. 'What will they think about me' is the greatest fear which kills many. Those who can fight this fear dies only once.
3. Self-comfort is the most essential component of living. We have fear of 'what they would think or say' because we are not confident and comfortable with our own self. Try to be at ease with your own self and live life fully.

## FOOD FOR THOUGHT

First we make our habits, then our habits make us.
– Charles C. Noble

# MINDSET

long with one of our family friends, we visited a place. On the way, we had to climb down. There were stairs. All adults (including me) started getting down through the stairs. But the children drifted away from us. They saw a place from where they can jump down. I asked them to come down through stairs. They said that they would prefer to jump. My friend said, "You all will fall down." They said, "No, we will not fall. You just watch." And one by one, they jumped. There was a little child of two and half years. They helped him too in jumping down holding his hand. They succeeded in their mission. We kept on watching.

## IN A NUTSHELL

1. If, like the children, we too try to jump from the 'closed, conventional thinking pattern', we can create great confidence within ourselves.
2. We try to discourage others because we are internally filled with fear. A lemon will give lemon juice, not mango juice. We shall present what we have inside. Thus, when we discourage others, we need to see whether we are filled with confidence or fear. If we are filled with fear, it is better to keep our mouth shut and work on ourselves rather than transfer the element of fear to others through our words of discouragement.

## FOOD FOR THOUGHT

*My greatest challenge has been to change the mindset of people. Mindsets play strange tricks on us. We see things the way our minds have instructed our eyes to see.*

–Muhammad Yunus

## PAIN IS GOOD

was having pain in my tooth and went to a dentist who said that I came at the right time as the problem in one tooth had started affecting the other teeth. I did not go to the dentist thinking about the damage the tooth would cause. I went because of pain. And the pain saved me from the damage to the other teeth also.

Once I received a complaint about my son from his teacher. I introspected and found out that I was not giving him quality time. I was being more mechanical rather than being compassionate. I developed compassion and started showering the same on him. The complaint helped to create a beautiful bond of compassion between us.

### IN A NUTSHELL

1. Pain helps us to identify the area of life where we need to give the balm of attention.
2. Sometimes one area can damage other areas. Immediate step needs to be taken to deal with the present pain area in order to save other areas from being damaged.
3. Pain     Introspection     Change     Gain

### FOOD FOR THOUGHT

*Although the world is full of suffering, it is also full of the overcoming of it.*

–Helen Keler

# END IS IMPORTANT

I was telling my son about an incident while he was having food. I was exaggerating each scene of the incident to make sure that the story ends only when he finishes the food. The incident was about my journey to Rajkot for a workshop. After listening to me for some time, he was not having the patience to wait. He asked, "Mamma, what happened at the end?" I said, "Dear, first listen to what happened next, then, gradually, we would reach the end". He started listening again. Then again he requested, "Mamma please, tell me what happened at the end." I found that his food was about to finish. So, I shared with him the end of the incident. He was relieved.

One day I came from a movie. My friend asked, "How was the movie?" I said, "Great!" She asked me to narrate the story. I was excited and wanted to tell her every detail. She stopped me midway and said, "What happened at the end?" See, even the adults are more concerned about the end. I thought that I watched the movie for entertainment. One hour was enough for my entertainment. Why did I sit for three hours? It was to know what happened at the end.

If we think further, a lot of hard-work, thinking, creativity, co-ordination are involved in the process to create the end product that is the movie itself. Probably each and every person in the movie is involved in the production process with great enthusiasm. The students who enjoy studies get happiness each day and then, the result is just a printout of their happiness. An employee of an organisation who enjoys each and every moment of his work gets the joy of every moment of working; the salary is just an extra part of his happiness.

---

### IN A NUTSHELL

1. *There are so many films that we start but they die as we do not give any end to it. There are so many journeys that we start, like exercising, writing a book, but the effort of the journey gets wasted as we do not give a proper end to it.*
2. *Process is very important, but ultimately it is the end that creates the actual motivation for the next process. End is a moment but*

process is a journey. So enjoying the process to get the pleasure of the end is the essence of journey in life.

3. When we leave from one place to another, no one says, "Happy ending" or "Happy destination", or "Happy goal"; each one wishes by saying, "Happy journey". Thus, life is a journey. One who can enjoy the journey, the destination would automatically be beautiful.

### FOOD FOR THOUGHT

*However beautiful the strategy, you should occasionally look at the results.*

—Winston Churchill

# WHERE ARE YOU?

had an appointment. I was on my way and was clueless on how to reach the place. I called up the concerned person to check the way. He asked me, "Where are you ma'am?" I said, "I exactly don't know but I am coming from Connaught Place." He again asked me, "But ma'am, where are you now?" I said, "I don't know." He said, "You first find out where are you. Then, I would be able to give you directions." I did so. I got down from my car. I took the details as to where I was. Then I again called up that person and this time telling my location to him became very easy. And my journey became very smooth.

### IN A NUTSHELL

1. First of all, we need to know where we are and then, design the pathway towards our destination.
2. It will be easier to get direction only when we know where we are.
3. Know your present weakness and strength, then plan your goal and design the direction to reach your self-growth.
4. It is much easier to locate a place when we have a map. Thus, we also need to create a fine map to reach the destination of happy relationship.

### FOOD FOR THOUGHT

*The first step towards getting somewhere is to decide that you are not going to stay where you are.*

—John Pierpont Morgan

# Hurdles

was there in a hurdle competition. The race started. The initial hurdles were very easy. Still many children who saw the subsequent hurdles backtracked from the race. The students, who were running, were seeing the present, crossed the present and reached the end. It seemed that the most difficult hurdle appeared to be very easy for these students.

### IN A NUTSHELL

1. Hurdles are part of life. The more we think, "What if! What if!", crossing the present situation would be extremely difficult. Thus, focusing on the present completely would help us to cross it more efficiently. This crossing would give us better skill to deal with future situations.
2. Initial difficulties may seem like 'hurdles'. The future difficulties would just be a situation to be handled.

### FOOD FOR THOUGHT

*If one has to become successful it is imperative that he works towards removing all the hurdles and obstacles coming in his way.*

—Rig Veda

# EFFECT OF COMPARISON

went to a company for conducting a workshop. There was a group of freshly appointed chemists and engineers. The chemists were very motivated to be appointed in a reputed company. They got clear instruction that for the next three months they would be getting stipend only. After that, they would be put on salary. They had no problem with the rule. But the problem started after they joined and found out that the engineers who were freshly appointed, having B.Tech degree, were getting salary from the day one of joining. The frustration became so obvious that they started expressing it in every workshop. The stipend versus salary became the main problem of their life.

### IN A NUTSHELL

1. When we proceed with our own objective, there is absolutely no problem. Once we start comparing, all sorts of feelings start bothering us.
2. Once we start comparing, the focus on our efforts and the spirit of enjoying the process goes down. This in the long run disturbs our growth. So we need to ignore minor issues to reach the major goal of our life. Comparison trap can be extremely dangerous and will destroy our self-esteem also.

### FOOD FOR THOUGHT

When you are content to be simply yourself and don't compare or compete, everybody will respect you."

–Lao Tzu

# **MASK**

There are many things which we ignore most of the time. But at times they can give us wonderful learning experiences. My friend's son met with an injury. I accompanied them to the hospital. There I noticed the doctors, nurses, ward boys, etc., putting on masks. The reason of putting on mask in a hospital is to protect oneself from germs. I also find that in Jainism, there is the practice of putting on mask. Here the intention is to save small insects from getting killed unknowingly (if they enter through the nose or mouth). The word personality originated from the word 'persona' meaning 'mask'. People of Greek were pioneers in drama and theatre. They used masks to perform different characters and bear a historical importance.

### IN A NUTSHELL

1. In real life, we put on several invisible masks. While keeping jealousy inside we put on the mask of concern. With corruption inside, we put on the mask of justice. These false masks have become so thick that those wearing such masks are unable to see their real self. More the inner core weakens, more will be the chances of us reaching the hospital where people around wear visible masks to avoid our germs infecting them.
2. On a daily basis we need to remove the invisible mask in order to lead a life of peace, happiness, and emotional security. The more the inner and outer alignment, the more would be the chance of inner peace.

### FOOD FOR THOUGHT

*1) Why do you wear a mask? Were you burned by acid or something? 2) Oh no. It's just they're terribly comfortable. I think everyone will be wearing them in the future.*
                                        *–The Princess Bride*

# CHANGE THE CHAIR

here was a workshop in a school. Before the workshop started, the principal of the school expressed her wish to change the chairs. But I found it rather strange as there was no need to change the furniture at that point of time. Moreover, the furniture was looking good and stable. Barely ten minutes later, when a participant got up his chair fell down. Then, I too got up to give some answer. My chair too fell down. This happened many times; I checked the legs of the chair and found that the back legs of the chair were not slanted. Therefore it was not able to withstand the push which one gives to the chair, while getting up.

### IN A NUTSHELL

1. Our thinking is based on the 'mental world' and therefore many misconceptions are possible. When the principal shared her desire to change chairs, I was finding it useless.
2. Like a chair needing a certain position to maintain its balance and not to fall, we too will need strong footing to balance ourselves from a fall as and when we get a push from the outside environment.

### FOOD FOR THOUGHT

*A mistake is to commit a misunderstanding.*

–Bob Dylan

# Conditional Vs Unconditional Communication

My friend was very upset that day. Her sister was getting engaged and she wanted to attend the function. She expressed this desire to her husband who said she could either go for the engagement or the marriage. He also threatened that if she went for the engagement, he would not accompany her and it would be embarrassing for her to answer the questions of relatives. My friend was in a dilemma with one part of her mind saying , "It is my right to attend my sister's engagement and marriage ceremony." The other part of mind saying, "I am upset as I am not getting any support from my husband. Let me control my emotions this time and enjoy the marriage ceremony. Argument and rigidity would ruin the situation and ruin my peace of mind." Emerging from the inner conflict, she decided not to attend the engagement and conveyed this to her husband. Her decision made the husband feel very ashamed about his conduct. Hiding feelings of guilt, he booked the journey tickets. Later both husband and wife jointly attended both the ceremonies. Who won? Maturity always wins.

### IN A NUTSHELL

1. When we use power to dominate others, it is our powerlessness that is showing up.
2. We generally break the bond and kill the emotions of other persons by putting conditions. Conditions may fulfill our demands, but may break the relationship.
3. I thought what impact he would have created if he communicated in the following way: "I understand your desire to go at this moment. But due to these reasons (if any), I was thinking will it be O.K. if we attend the marriage and not go at the engagement? Think about it and I am open to what you decide."
4. Restricting the EGO always leads to happiness and peace within self and in relationship.

### FOOD FOR THOUGHT

*If we are strong, our strength will speak for itself. If we are weak, words will be of no help.*

—John Fitzgerald Kennedy

# BEING IN TUNE WITH ONE SELF

went to a school for a workshop. A teacher was playing flute nicely. While playing the flute, he was adjusting his distance from the mike time to time ; sometimes he would come near the mike depending on the volume of sound he wanted to create. I found this to and fro motion very rhythmic and melodious. When the pitch was high, he would move away from the mike; when the pitch was low, he will come closer to the mike. Everyone enjoyed the melodious performance. When we also wish to listen to certain radio station, we need to tune exactly at the right frequency. If we don't, we would not be able to enjoy the melody. The untuned noise would only generate further irritation.

## IN A NUTSHELL

1. *When we know when to maintain distance from what, we can take the best out of our life. For example, if I have conflict with someone, I need to create some distance with that person (even in my thoughts), and then, again go near to resolve the conflict. But if we remain close to the conflict and criticise the person to every next person, it will increase the problem.*
2. *The flute player was blocking a few holes of the flute allowing free flow of air from other holes so that melodious tune comes out. For peak performance, blocking few activities for a period of time is essential. For example, to complete this book, I need to block certain areas, like watching T.V. or making regular visits to friends. Then, when I am through with my work, I can go back to them to bring out the best tune of my life.*

## FOOD FOR THOUGHT

*All a man can betray is his conscience.*

—Joseph Conrad

# *Power of Similarity*

was conducting a workshop in Chandigarh. It was a two-day workshop. A lady was listening to me with great attentivenness and I could sense her respect for me in her eyes, right from the very beginning. She was displaying a strong feeling of bonding with me. The workshop got over successfully and she came up to me during the valedictory programme and said, "Ma'am, I am also a Bengali." There was a sense of connectivity in her voice. I must know, how I struggled for a full hour at the start of the session to create that connectivity with the audience, and how can she be an exception!

## IN A NUTSHELL

1. There is tremendous power in 'sense of similarity'. Whenever we find that the other person likes the same food that we love or admires same hero whom we admire, an immediate 'feeling of belongingness' gets created.
2. If we can create a power of similarity knowing that we all are similar in terms of being 'human', we can grow in real sense.
3. A good salesperson is a good relationship manager. Using the 'power of similarity' is one of their powerful skills.

## FOOD FOR THOUGHT

*Love is the power to see similarity in the dissimilar.*
—Theodor Adorno

# NO END

veryone wants a beautiful end and no one wants to hear 'no' from others. In a workshop where I was invited as a trainer, the participants were from different parts of Haryana. The organisers were concerned about the smooth ENDing of the workshop. The principal of the school was quite relaxed. He said that end would be good as END means 'EFFORT NEVER DIES'. He was sure that as he had put in the right effort and it would certainly have a winning END.

In the meantime I needed colour printout of some documents. I checked with a teacher for the same. She said that there was 'no' provision of coloured printout in the school. I was slightly upset which probably reflected on my face. The principal again added, "Don't worry. It will be done as NO means there must be NEXT OPPORTUNITY." He got it done from the nearby market.

## IN A NUTSHELL

1. Once we focus on the effort, the end is bound to be beautiful.
2. If someone denies our request, it means that we have another opportunity to look for better prospect.

## FOOD FOR THOUGHT

*Luck is what happens when preparation meets opportunity.*
—Seneca

# *Real Present*

was into a difficult phase of my life, struggling hard to come out of my shell of sadness. All my friends assured that they are with me. My parents came to me immediately. They stayed with me till the time I was able to come out of my shell. One of my friends, Vibha and Anita, paid frequent visits to my place. They were in constant touch with me over phone. But it was the personal presence that gave me more comfort than phone calls.

### IN A NUTSHELL

1. Nothing could give me as much comfort as the presence of my parents and my friends. This was because 'PRESENCE IS THE MOST PRECIOUS PRESENT'.
2. Today technology is helping us to 'keep in touch' but the effect of 'real TOUCH' is getting lost.
3. Support with physical presence can bring 'life' in life of others.

### FOOD FOR THOUGHT

*Absence sharpens love, presence strengthens it.*
—Benjamin Franklin

## PUT DOWN YOUR DARK GOGGLES

e were travelling from one place to other. A young girl who was working with me was putting on goggles. In the evening, she was not able to see the road with clarity. She removed her goggles and kept it in the 'goggles box'. She said, "I was wondering why I was not able to see clearly. I forgot I was putting on goggles."

### IN A NUTSHELL

1. Till the goggle was working fine for her, the young girl was using it. Once it was not working, she removed it and kept it safe for future use. Thus, if any of our thought, assumptions and belief is not bringing the desired result, we need to check whether we require them or we need to keep them aside for a certain period.
2. Remove our goggles of old belief and see the world with better clarity.
3. When she found darkness, she did not realise that darkness is due to her own goggles. Removing the dark goggles brought light. Similarly, when we are in dark, we need to check whether we are putting on invisible dark goggles of some faulty belief system.

### FOOD FOR THOUGHT

We are limited, not by our abilities, but by our vision.

## POWER OF OPTIONISTIC ATTITUDE

An employee in an organisation did not get promotion. He was very disappointed. He called me up. I said, "Try hard." He answered, "Nivedita, you don't know how much I work hard. I stay late. When no one is ready to work, I work. But still my fate is not supporting me." I found lot of negativity and hopelessness in his words. I said, "I don't know what you mean by hard work, but I would say you can practise possibility thinking with 'optionistic attitude'." After a month, he called me up and said, "Nivedita, the 'optionistic attitude' has changed my life. I am balanced and I am getting positive feedback. Actually, I realised that I was working for promotion and not for my satisfaction. My 'optionistic attitude' was dead. Now, whenever I am in a difficult situation, I ask myself 'what option I have now?' It has really worked for me. Whether there is any other option or not, I always have the option to be happy."

### IN A NUTSHELL

1. "Be optimistic", "Be positive" are the words which we hear frequently, on how to be optimistic, we rarely get a course. "Possibility thinking" is a very powerful tool to be optimistic and positive. Think "How can I make it possible?"
2. To be positive, think about the various options available. Then you would find that your mind automatically shifting from 'problem-based thinking' to 'solution-based thinking.'

### FOOD FOR THOUGHT

*When a person acts without knowledge of what he thinks, feels, needs or wants, he does not yet have the option of choosing to act differently."*

–Clark Moustakas

# POWER OF HOPE AND DAMAGE OF HOPE MANIPULATION

I was working as a trainer for a firm. I was a regular visitor there and was familiar with the behaviour pattern of the people there. Samina was an enthusiastic worker. She worked very hard. I never heard her saying 'no' to any work. She always remained positive with a high level of energy. For three years, I observed her the same way. She was genuinely a person with high energy. But the fourth year, I found a great change. I was sitting in her manger's room. The manager called her and asked her to do some work. She refused and said, "Sir, I cannot do. I am doing some other work." The manager insisted that she should complete the task urgently. But she refused and went away. The manager said that she had changed and become arrogant. I was also able to see her aggression. But I felt something was hidden behind. I thought of having lunch with her. She shared her frustration. Her husband is working in Rampur where this organisation has its branch. She wants to get shifted there. Since three years she has been requesting for the same. But every year she gets the same assurance that she would be shifted but nothing happened. Now, she has given up. She has realised that these people will not let her go. She has lost her faith in these people. When I asked the manager, he said that he could not let her leave as she was an efficient worker and he would not get a substitute for her. But since then, I never saw her working sincerely. The organisation lost an enthusiastic and energetic worker.

### IN A NUTSHELL

1. Hope brings energy. Breaking of hope brings the end to living.
2. Manipulating hope would lead to violence. If we promise something, it generates hope in other person. Breaking that hope would break the soft heart of the person leading to de-motivation and frustration in every aspect of life.

## FOOD FOR THOUGHT

*Hope doesn't come from calculating whether the good news is winning out over the bad. It's simply a choice to take action.*
—Anna Lappe

## THOMAS EDISON ALSO FAILED 1000 TIMES

had a counseling session for a young man. He was running his own business. Every time he failed, he said, "So what? Edison also failed so many times!" And thus, he kept on facing failures with a positive attitude. But after the 19th failure, he got frustrated and said, "Ma'am, Edison also failed. I am also failing. But I am not able to bear the failure any more. What is the difference?" I said, "There is a vast difference. The problem is that Edison tried and failed. Then, he learnt the reason why he failed. He then started with new energy and again failed. Then, he again learnt the reason of failing. This learning gave him motivation, and the 'feeling of failure' was not able to crush his energy. He never repeated the same mistake. His goal was the same. But he changed his pathways. This is the difference."

### IN A NUTSHELL

1. Failing is not a problem, but having a 'fear of failure' is a matter of concern. So, change the 'failure' episode to 'learning opportunity event'.
2. Analysing failure is important for effective learning. Then, applying the learning in future planning is the second most important step.

### FOOD FOR THOUGHT

*The greatest barrier to success is the fear of failure.*
—Sven Goran Eriksson

## SYMPATHY SEEKER VS CURE SEEKER

went to a boutique. I could see a spark in the face of the lady who was in-charge of the boutique. Her face was glowing. Physically too she looked fine. As part of the process of learning from experience, I asked her, "What is the secret of your physical fitness?" She said, "I am a cure seeker." I couldn't understand. But I felt something is hidden. I asked her what she meant by 'cure seeker'. She said, "Whenever I have any physical, financial or emotional problem, I think about cure. I have some liver related problem, which the doctor said would stay with me throughout my life". This was the secret of her health. She was a 'cure seeker' and not a 'sympathy seeker'.

### IN A NUTSHELL

1. Sympathy does not cure the problem, rather strengthens the pain. Moreover, it gives a license that the pain is valid.
2. The cure seeker would have unlimited horizon to move. Sympathy seeker would be stuck in a small dark room.
3. Sympathy seeking attitude kills a person's thinking to move forward in life. It closes the vision to see the positive side of life. Sympathy seeking makes a person emotionally blind.

### FOOD FOR THOUGHT

*Real freedom is creative, proactive, and will take me into new territories. I am not free if my freedom is predicated on reacting to my past.*

–Kenny Loggins

## EFFECTIVE DRIVING

When I started driving, I was happily waiting for the day when I would call myself a perfect driver. I used to wait for the day when I would drive while talking to others. And the day came when I realised that I learnt to drive effectively. I felt that the day has come when I could be relaxed while driving. When did the anxiety of gear-change, monitoring clutch, break, etc., vanished, I did not realise. One day, while I was driving, someone came from the wrong side. Thank God! I was able to see it at the right time. I slowed down and saved myself from an accident. I realised that from now onwards I needed to be more alert. I needed to foresee the mistake of others to save myself as well as others.

### IN A NUTSHELL

1. Just as effective driving is about saving yourself and others by foreseeing others' mistakes while driving, similarly, effective talking is not about just knowing words, but actually knowing the use of words and knowing when to give a pause. It is about analysing others' mistakes and then, designing response.
2. Major road accidents are caused by the people who think themselves to be 'perfect driver'. Similarly, major relationship accidents are created by those who think 'only' themselves to be perfect in every situation.
3. As mental balance is needed to become a perfect driver, similarly mental balance is also required to be an effective driver of relationship and life.

### FOOD FOR THOUGHT

*Patience is something you admire in the driver behind you, but not in one ahead.*

—Bill McGlashen

# *Feeling Vs Showing*

Right from childhood, we are all taught to stand up with respect when the National Anthem is sung. That day, I was going somewhere with my friend. In a park a group of children were singing the National Anthem. My friend immediately stopped and stood attentively. I also stood with her on the side of the road. All were looking at us. A few crossed the road and a few others stood with us. After that incident, I developed a conditioned response that whenever I hear the National Anthem, my soul prods my body to stand up in attention.

## IN A NUTSHELL

1. We keep on being conscious on 'what will others think'. Actual confidence comes when we develop courage to do what we think is right. Then, the world salutes us.
2. Feeling of respect is more important than showing respect.
3. Fighting the fear of judgment is the most important step for moving towards success.

## FOOD FOR THOUGHT

*Courage is doing what you're afraid to do. There can be no courage unless you're scared.*

—Eddie Rickenbacker

## PATIENCE VS TOLERANCE

went to a function. While sitting, I found that an acquaintance of mine was also there. She came and sat near me. The function was yet to start. Probably she was searching for somebody to pour her heart out. After being seated, she said, "Nivedita, I want to ask you a question." I looked at her and gave her the nod to continue. She asked, "How long can one keep patience?" I realised that something was boiling inside her. I asked, "But in what context do you need to have patience?" She said, "I am telling my husband to give time to family, but he does not care. He is there on tour and when he is at home, he is there with his phone." I said, "Dear, I feel you are tolerating, but not having enough patience. When you tolerate, you are suppressing your feelings. And it has a risk of damaging your relationships as well as your health." Immediately she blurted out, "Yes, I am getting furious on my daughter these days." I continued, "In patience, you share your feelings, take steps to deal with the situation, without being anxious of the result." She said, "That means, I need to share my feelings to my husband without forcing him to change, so that, if he is not fulfilling my expectations, I don't spoil my relationship with him as well as my daughter. I think this makes sense. I am wasting my life to change the other person and wasting my energy too. Yes, you are right, I am tolerating but I don't have patience."

### IN A NUTSHELL

1. Patience gives a feeling of calmness; tolerance gives a feeling of anxiety.
2. Patience gives growth, tolerance generates frustration.
3. Nothing sorts out on its own. We need to take steps with calm state of mind, rather than trying to 'feel big' by saying 'I am tolerating'.
4. 'Tolerating' is basically a mask that we put on to our 'fear of failure' and a sign of handling situations less effectively.

### FOOD FOR THOUGHT

*Our patience will achieve more than our force.*
—Edmund Burke

# *Weakness Vs Way for Improvement*

nita is a good, thoughtful, and helpful friend of mine. One day, when I went to her house, she was talking about her son. She said, "He is improving by being more interactive". When I looked at her son I was able to see a spark in his face, when he heard this statement from his mother. He was extremely happy.

## IN A NUTSHELL

1. Weakness becomes a never changing brand, while way for improvement is like designing a brand.
2. Weakness gives a negative feeling, while way for improvement gives a positive feeling.
3. Weakness is 'trait oriented', while 'way for improvement' is 'action oriented'.
4. Thus, 'weakness' will pull us down, make us feel low, while 'way for improvement' would make us proceed upwards, feel high.
5. 'Way for improvement' gives us a scope to 'W' on it, that is to 'work on it' and then to 'W' over it, that is 'Win' over the weakness. Thus, one W (Way for improvement) leads to two other powerful W's (Work and Win).

## FOOD FOR THOUGHT

*There is one corner of the universe you can be certain of improving, and that's your own self.*

—Aldous Huxley

## *Similarity Attracts*

was conducting a training workshop in a renowned company in Gurgaon. We were having lunch break. After lunch, I was coming back to the assigned training room. On my way, I found four individuals sitting together and reading a newspaper. I proceeded further and found two individuals moving towards a person having a cigarette in his hand. These two individuals also joined him for smoking. I came inside the room. I found three individuals sitting together. No one was talking to one another, but each one of them was busy sending and receiving messages through their mobile. These people were together on the basis of what they were. They were attracting same kind of people. I thought, what kind of people I want to attract: yes, certainly positive, happy people. To attract them, I need to be the same. It sounds great!

### IN A NUTSHELL

1. In science, opposites attract. But in life, similarities attract.
2. Each one attracts people with similar intentions and thought process.
3. Think about what kind of people you wish to be around you. Be the same. Your desire would automatically be fulfilled.

### FOOD FOR THOUGHT

*Love is the power to see similarity in dissimilar.*
—Theodor Adorno

## PRINCIPAL WITH PRINCIPLES

I went to a workshop in Jammu. I was impressed by the leadership qualities of the principal. I saw him calling one of the teachers to his room. The teacher entered the room with a broad smile as if he was sure to get a reward. And he was right. The principal said, "I am very happy the way you were teaching Physics. I don't have science background, but I too learnt the concept you taught." Saying this, he took out a 'congrats' card and handed over to him. Soon after, I found him calling another teacher. He handed over a 'thank you' card and said, "I appreciate your extra effort made in helping the child to cope with Maths. He passed just because of you. Thank you so much." I was not able to control my curiosity. I asked, "From where do you get the feedback on performance? Do you call only those who do good work? Or do you also call those who need some improvement?" He replied, "Let me answer your first question. I sometimes sit in the class or sometimes observe the class from my monitor attached to the classroom camera. Now, your second question. Yes, I only call those teachers who show some positivity in their performance. They in turn share why they got the card in the next day's morning assembly. This gives positive learning to the whole environment. Everyone does depict some or the other positive traits. So, it is my task to create an environment of motivation by focusing on the positive qualities of each of them."

### IN A NUTSHELL

1. *What do you want to see? Focus more on that.*
2. *We are generally complaining about what we don't want and then, we attract them more. The result of this mentality is dissatisfaction. To increase the satisfaction level, let's start seeing what would give us satisfaction. And we would attract them more into our life.*
3. *Criticism is easy. But appreciation needs real courage. So, increase your courage by creating a vision to see what you can appreciate. Can you appreciate something while you are reading this book? Start now.*

### FOOD FOR THOUGHT

A man is usually more careful of his money than he is of his principles.

—Plato

## SATISFACTION DILEMMA

am a person who believes in healthy living. So, vegetable soup is an indispensable part of my daily routine. That day, one of my friends came to visit me. I served her vegetable soup. My friend was somehow reluctant to take the soup as she was not very comfortable with its taste. I said, "Dear, the vegetable soup of gourd is so delicious to drink. After drinking it, you will feel satisfied as your body would be getting something very nutritious. Moreover, I too will feel satisfied to serve you with a nutritious drink." My son immediately replied, "Yes, even I would be very satisfied as I would have less amount of soup as my share." My son does not like soup. He takes the soup only as medicine.

### IN A NUTSHELL

1. We all have our own limited horizons of thinking. We tend to see things through an invisible spectacle which is fitted into our brain system. Thus, the processing of information for each one of us is also different. Misunderstanding would occur if we do not understand the value of information processing.
2. Children speak directly. My son does not like to drink soup. It is a blessing for him if his share gets reduced. Thus, he expressed his area of satisfaction level. In our daily lives, we need to re-check whether our area of satisfaction matches with others' area of satisfaction so that we remain in the same platform of satisfaction.

### FOOD FOR THOUGHT

No man or woman is an island. Existence as a lonely self is meaningless. You can achieve maximum satisfaction when you feel related to some greater purpose in life, something greater than yourself.

–Denis Waitley

## LAUGHING CAN BE PAINFUL

rati was working on the computer with extreme concentration. Her friend Kalpana came and said something. Arati's response showed that she did not like Kalpana's interference. Sensing her displeasure, Kalpana said, "Arati, I was just joking." Another person said, "Yes, I think you need to announce in advance that you are going to joke!"

### IN A NUTSHELL

1. Tone will speak for itself whether a person is joking or not. But it is also important to know the mindset of the person at the receiving end. If the person at the receiving end is not in a mood to receive the message, there would be visible or hidden conflict.
2. It is important to know how to speak and it is also important to know the 'mindset of others' before we speak.

### FOOD FOR THOUGHT

Better to understand a little than to misunderstand a lot.
— Anonymous

## *Realistic Optimism*

received a call from Mr. Shammi Sukh to remind me about a workshop in his organisation. He too is an author. He is also a good friend and mentor to me. He informed me that he had completed his 'dream book' and submitted it to a publisher. The manuscript was under process. Then I asked more about the book. He said, "It is under process. I am waiting for its acceptance." I said, "I am waiting for the book." He said, "Actually you are more optimistic." Till this book of mine got accepted by my publisher, I received his book – "Make your Life a Great Experience".

---

### IN A NUTSHELL

1. *Optimism says, "Everything will be great." Realistic optimism says, "I have put in right kind of effort at the right time. So, things would be great." It is good to be optimistic, but it is important to have realistic optimism.*
2. *Visualisation is a great technique to achieve success. I practice it not only for my success, but also for the success of others as well.*

---

### FOOD FOR THOUGHT

*I can't change the direction of the wind, but I can adjust my sails to always reach my destination.*

–Jimmy Dean

## *POWER OF PASSIONATE WORK*

was having a telephone talk with a person who is also into writing. I said, "What next sir?" He said, "Rest". It was slightly shocking to me. I said, "Is this the name of your next book?" He said, "No, actually I have been writing books for the last 18 years. Now for the next two years I need a break." I said, "Great thought! But let me see how long can you stop writing."

I again got a call from him, after 15 days. He said, "Nivedita, you were right. I was feeling restless due to my over-rest. I have started writing again and feeling better now".

### IN A NUTSHELL

1. Habit is a mindset which creates a pattern. Positive habit needs to be cherished; negative habit needs to be re-conditioned into desired habit.
2. Each one creates a social identity through his 'working pattern'. Think about what social identity have you created. Is it "Mr./ Mrs. ….. cannot sit idle" or "What happened today? Mr/ Mrs. ……. is working!

### FOOD FOR THOUGHT

*Men's natures are alike; it is their habits that separate them.*

## EARNING FROM LEARNING

My son is a fantastic learner. One day I was making lemonade. He asked me, "I will prepare. You just teach me the methods of making it so that I can learn." Whenever any mechanic will come, he will be the first one to provide assistance (whether the person needs or not). One day I asked, "Why do you wish to learn everything?" He said, "See, when I grow big, I can become a chef. If there are many chefs and no vacancy for me, I can become a scientist as I love to learn science experiments. If this area is also filled, then I can become an artist as I am good in drawing and craft work. If that area is blocked, I can become a magician and earn." I thought, "Little boy of 10 years and such great thoughts."

### IN A NUTSHELL

1. Learning has the element of earning in the word - L-EARNING. Thus, a person willing to learn is endowed with the opportunity to earn.
2. Crisis never comes announcing it. Thus, a well-learnt skill could help in earning in a moment of crisis.
3. Start learning from now on. If someone asks you about the gift you want, just ask the person what he can teach you. That would be the best gift that would always remain with you.

### FOOD FOR THOUGHT

*A happy life is one spent in learning, earning and yearning.*
—Lillian Gish

## Magic of Two Ears

went to a company where I was sitting in the room of the General Manager (GM). A young lady came and complained about someone. The GM listened thoroughly and said, "I understand your problem. Let me see how I can help you." He did not react or blame anyone. After she left, he called the person about whom the complaint was made. He listened to his point of view too and refrained from making any negative comments about him on the basis of the complaint. He said, "Fine, I understand your point of view." Then he started talking to me. I asked, "Now what sir?" He said, "I shall think and see how I can develop a healthy relation between them. They need to work together. So, they need to have positive professional relationship." I liked his approach.

### IN A NUTSHELL

1. We have two ears. It is meant to listen to the point of view of both sides. If we only listen to one side view, it would destroy the relationship in some way or the other.
2. In between two ears, there is a 'brain' for processing of what goes inside our ear. If we are using the ear ignoring the power of the processing system, it would again inflict damage.

### FOOD FOR THOUGHT

*Nothing that is worth knowing can be taught.*

–Oscar Wilde

# Mis-Take

learn many things from children. One day, I was watching a few children playing. A team lost due to the mistake of a child. The teammates started yelling at him. He was quiet. I was feeling sorry for that little boy. I continued watching the game to know its outcome. The second match started and the team won. I noticed that the boy who was blamed for the lapse had become very alert throughout the game. I could not resist myself and went to the child and asked, "I saw you playing both the matches. I found a difference. I found that you were more energetic and alert during the second part of the game, although you were criticised. How?" He said, "I simply played in the fi rst place. But my team lost because of my casual approach and I understood the mistake. Next time, I took the game seriously, not casually." This little boy's answer was an eye-opener to me on many things:

### IN A NUTSHELL

1. When there is a mis-take, we need to 'take' a u-turn and remove the 'mis' and take it as an opportunity to grow. Change mistake to Miss Take (Taking opportunity)

### FOOD FOR THOUGHT

It was when I found out I could make mistakes that I knew I was on to something.

—Ornette Coleman

# Right Spectacle

went for a workshop. There was another faculty professor with me. He took out his spectacles to read something. Immediately after putting on the spectacles, he said, "Oh God! I have brought my wife's spectacles." He was not able to read a single word. The faculty had difficulty as he was supposed to read certain exercises. He took my help to read. But as he was not able to do self-reading, he was feeling uncomfortable throughout.

## IN A NUTSHELL

1. To read correctly, we need the right kind of spectacles. Similarly, we also need right kind of perceptive power to read a situation well. When we read the situation well, we can respond well to the situation. If we cannot, we will mishandle the situation.
2. When the person was carrying the spectacles, he was under the impression that he picked up the right one. But only when he used it, he was able to realise that the spectacles were of use only for his wife and useless for him.
3. It also might have caused problem for his wife. Thus, pick up the information which you really require and leave out those you don't require, without criticism. May be, it would be of use to others.

## FOOD FOR THOUGHT

"Miracles happen everyday. Change your perception on what a miracle is and you'll see them all around you."
—Jon Bon Jovi

## MAGIC OF ENHANCING SELF-ESTEEM

Mr. Anil was working as a supervisor for the cleaning staff and was fed up with their attitude and always complained: "They always want to save their skin." When Anil went on leave for two weeks, Mr. Kaushik was given the same responsibility. The latter was very happy with the same group. What was the difference? Mr. Anil showed his staff what they did wrong. Mr. Kaushik enhanced their self-esteem by showing them what they did right. He appreciated them when they reached on time or cleaned something nicely, or performed any other task with dedication. He praised them in public. This created a feeling of 'want to work' and not 'have to work'. The relationship between Mr. Anil and the workers were horrible. On the other hand, the relationship between Mr. Kaushik and the same group of workers were wonderful.

### IN A NUTSHELL

1. Many people do a job under force or due to situational factors. For such kind of people, self-esteem needs to be boosted in order to get a 'taste of success'.
2. When we drive we obviously focus on where we want to go, not towards the railing where we don't want to go. Similarly, we need to focus on what we wish to see, rather than on what we don't want to see.

### FOOD FOR THOUGHT
*Someone's opinion of you does not have to become your reality.*
—Les Brown

## NOT AT THE COST OF MENTAL PEACE

It was vacation time for me. I planned my personal and professional trip together. I had six destinations to visit within a month. Three were some e-tickets and three computerised railway tickets. I had kept the computerised tickets in the *almirah* very safely. I was relaxed and assumed that they are safe. Suddenly there was a change in the schedule of the first destination. I needed to re-plan. Getting ticket was a major problem. It was May 2010, getting tickets in *tatkal* was too difficult. I had given the responsibility to one of my acquaintances. But there was a certain anxiety regarding the ticket. My whole internal system was focused on the work being done. Finally the job was done. I was extremely relaxed. I did all my packing as per a checklist– separate gift bag for relatives; separate food bag for my son; workshop material; laptop; variety of clothes; work baggage for waiting time, etc. According to me, I had done wonderful packing based on my planning. It was time to leave Delhi. I left Delhi with a relaxed mind, assuming zero problems. I had taken each and everything with me starting from pin, brush to laptop. I boarded the train, and after a small chat with my son, went to sleep. Immediately my sub-conscious mind got activated. Remember the tickets in the *almirah*? It is still lying there. I felt like taking the train back to Delhi, going back home to bring the tickets and erase all unevenness. But life moves forward according to its own plan. Similarly, train also has to proceed forward according to schedules. So, I stopped fooling myself and started thinking about options. The situation was complex as my key was in my neighbour's place and their key was in someone else's place. These are the moments of crisis when you realise how much quality and time you have invested in personal relationship. I thought about one best option and two backup options. Honestly, sleep was getting disturbed. What if no plan works? I knew that if we become too anxious with certain plan, the anxiety would block the work getting done. So, I thought about the worst that could happen. The worst would be that I would lose Rs. 15,000/-. No choice. It is better to lose Rs.15,000/- rather than losing approximately 28,800 seconds (8 hours) of my sleep. And each lost second would then create damage to my internal system. This self-talk worked. Money would come back, but this night would not. Moreover, I also said to myself, "Nivedita, everyone can sleep well when things are going fine, but the actual challenge is to sleep well when things are not moving well." I put a challenge to my sub-conscious and went to sleep. Amazing, I woke up when my son asked me for his toothbrush. Then the mission to work according to my plan started and by evening 4.30 p.m., the mission of getting the tickets out my house was successful. Then, getting it couriered was a small bit of work left, on which I was very confident.

### IN A NUTSHELL

1. In a difficult situation, rather than wasting time and energy on wasteful and worrisome thoughts, it is important to focus on two most important questions: 'what can I do now' and 'when can I take the required steps'. For me, I focused on my sleep and then, continued with the necessary steps the next morning. It was of no use to waste whole night worrying.

2. Work on your relationship when there is no rain so that when it rains, you can feel comfortable and relaxed. Social support is the biggest source of 'mental peace'. Work on them on a daily basis.

### FOOD FOR THOUGHT

*Acceptance of others, their looks, their behaviours, their beliefs can bring an inner peace and tranquility in you – instead of anger and resentment.*

–Unknown

## JUDGING AND MIS-JUDGING

It was during the same personal cum professional trip I made – my first visit to Tatanagar. My ticket was booked in *Tatkal* with great difficulty, for Purushottam Express of 31 May 10. I sat in the train with great relief. Train was supposed to reach Tatanagar on 1 June 10 at 8.20 p.m. Train was on time. Around 11.00 a.m. on 1 June, I noticed that a person sitting near me was deeply probing the Railway guide. He seemed to be making a plan, with his wife, on where to get down – Kharagpur or Adra. My mind started judging them. How ridiculous is this? They are making plans at the last moment? They seem to be educated but such irresponsibility? But then, I jerked myself and said, "Nivedita, stop judging others and focus on what you need to do now?" Thinking this, I started talking to my son. Around 1.00 p.m., I asked the waiter about the time the train would be reaching Tatanagar. The person who was engrossed in talking to the Railway guide interrupted and said, "Ma'am, this train probably would not go to Tatanagar. But don't worry. We would get down at Kharagpur. If you wish, you can join us." I felt, "Oh God! The person about whom I was making a judgment of being irresponsible was actually at an 'advanced crisis planning'. He was even able to comfort other passengers as he had already prepared himself to face the crisis situation.

### IN A NUTSHELL

1. Rather than focusing and trying to correct the 'mistakes' of others, we need to correct our 'mistake finding attitude'.
2. A person who can foresee the difficult situation and mentally deal with that difficulty can easily handle any situation in real life too.
3. By creating a powerful 'mental framework', we can also become a source of strength for others to emerge as a 'natural leader'.

### FOOD FOR THOUGHT

*Judgements prevent us from seeing the good that lies beyond appearances.*

—Wayne Dyer

## FEAR – THE WORST ENEMY

was having a workshop in Indore. I was staying in one of the best hotels, considered to be three-star. Since my workshop was scheduled for the next day, I was doing my work and enjoying the time. Time went by… It was 9.00 p.m. I went to the washroom to brush my teeth. As soon I put on the light I saw a long tail moving under the light-box. I was not able to see its body and could not confirm whether it was a snake or a lizard. I was really scared. I called the room service people. When I was saying, "I saw a tail….", they were able to see the fear on my face. I did not say anything else. They called up somebody and said, "We need to change the room for ma'am." I was thinking, they could have done their job of removing the snake/lizard even without changing my room. But instead they shifted me to another room and then, removed the big lizard, which they communicated to me later. Shifting the room also changed my emotional state from that of fear to a relaxed state of being.

### IN A NUTSHELL

1. *We cannot fake our emotions as emotions can leak. I was having fear of the insect and the house-keeping was having fear of my fear. Thus, we didn't use many words as our emotions were speaking through our facial expression and body language. Words can fake, but reflection of emotions is always genuine.*
2. *They shifted me to another room and then worked on the issue. When we are in some intense negative emotion, we need to change our focus, to become relaxed so that we can work on the issue effectively.*
3. *In a moment of crisis rather than explaining facts we need to address the emotions and provide comfort. That would create a beautiful and long lasting relationship. You would find a journey of beautiful relations resulting from positive emotions of love, trust, compassion, and support during the moments of crisis.*

### FOOD FOR THOUGHT

Nothing in life is to be feared. It is only to be understood.
—Marie Curie

# Voices and Expressing Your Voice

Fear gripped all when a train was attacked by Naxalites in May 2010. I happened to travel towards the same area, barely two days after the incident. My destination was Tatanagar and I took the Purushottam express. Tickets were issued by the railway authorities an hour before the departure of the train. But at the last moment, the railway authorities announced that the train would not go till Tatanagar but would be diverted. And it was diverted at Adra. The passengers explored many options on what to do. Some were heard criticising the railway department. In between one person got up and said, "Why not we talk to the superintendent of the station? Maybe something works!" All obliged him as if he had some magnetic power. When they expressed their grievance, the railway authorities said that it was not possible to make any alternate arrangement. This agitated a few of the passengers who pulled the chain when the train started. Finally, the railway authorities promised to make special arrangements in Adra. When we got down at Adra, we were informed that a passenger train has been arranged but it will not go to Tatanagar. It will drop us in Sini. Some started boarding Purushottam planning to wait at Kharagpur station the whole night to board another train in the morning. I was also about to get into Purushottam. But soon a young girl, Anisha, who was doing Mass Communication said, "Aunty, let's go to the passenger train. At least, we would move forward. There are many people with us." Probably, my internal system was longing for such directional instruction. Immediately, another uncle-aunty said, "No beta, come back, we will wait at Kharagpur in the night. At least till then, we would be in the AC compartment." Where to go?" Anisha's words seemed persuasive for me. Her courage inspired me and I moved forward with her. Yes, when we boarded the passenger train, the train authorities informed that train would not go to Tatanagar. Passengers knew now how to get the job done. Rather than talking first, they pulled the chain. Promise was made that another train would be arranged at Sini. But when the train reached Sini Railway people said they had no information on any arrangement supposedly made. They said, "You people have been fooled." This statement hurt the self-esteem of all. Now, they were firm that they would not allow the passenger train to move forward until some arrangement was made. After a lot of altercation, arrangement was made. Passengers were shouting that they would take money back in Tatanagar for their physical and mental harassment. At last we reached Tatanagar at 2.30 a.m on 2 June instead of 1 June at 8.30 p.m, some 6 hours behind the scheduled time. Not bad. But when the passengers saw their long waiting relatives at the station, their anger vanished. They even forgot the matter of getting the money refunded. All were too anxious to reach home as early as possible.

## IN A NUTSHELL

1. There were two voices – Anisha's and uncle-aunt's. One voice was the 'voice of courage'; other the 'voice of comfort'. I had a choice to make. Following the voice of courage would give me present pain but permanent future power. On the other hand, following the voice of comfort would give me present pleasure but would not give me any power for future. I chose the voice of courage as I thought that I would reach my destination by expanding my horizon of comfort.
2. Articulating or expressing the feeling helps the other person to know what we wish. In most cases, it is found that we crib more internally rather than expressing our desire in the appropriate manner .
3. When people reached their destination, their aggression vanished. Reaching the destination erased all pain. Thus, when someone is being aggressive; show patience. When he reaches the destination his aggression will vanish.

## FOOD FOR THOUGHT

*Self-expression must pass into communication for its fulfillment.*
—Pearl S. Buck

# RE-FRAMING

was in a training. The introduction session was in progress. One participant asked me, "How much qualified are you?" I said, "I am not much qualified." He was shocked to get such response. I asked him, "Did you get the desired point from my answer?" He said, "No". I said, "I gave you an answer according to your question, but still the answer was meaningless for you." Then, I told him to re-frame the question accordingly to elicit the response he desired. He said, "OK ma'am, what is your qualification?" I now replied, "I am a Doctorate in Psychology."

## IN A NUTSHELL

1. Rather than getting frustrated for not getting the desired consequence, we can use the power of choice to re-frame our response.
2. Once we know our goal and find it difficult to reach through a particular way don't change the goal. Just search for alternative ways to reach the same goal. Rather than finding your goal accomplishment to be impossible, think 'how can I make it possible.'

### FOOD FOR THOUGHT

*When you are through changing, you are through.*

–Bruce Barton

## CONFIDENCE Vs OVERCONFIDENCE

met a person who was going for a group discussion. I asked him to do some practice. Being a trainer, I was ready to help him. He said, "I don't need any practice." I asked, "Why do you think that you require no practice?" He said, "I know I only will win." There was a force on 'I only'. I again said, "I think some amount of practice would make you more confident." He said, "I am already confident." I realised it was meaningless to convert a conversation into an argument. I kept quiet and waited for the result. He went for the group discussion and could not perform well. He came out and said, "The judges are not up to the mark. They do not know how to judge. I was the best." And I felt, for him, no one could ever become a perfect judge.

### IN A NUTSHELL

1. *Confidence says, "With right kind of effort at the right time would bring success." Overconfidence says, "Whether I put in effort or not, I only will win."*
2. *Confidence focuses on I + E + E (Internal ability + Effort + Environmental factors). Overconfidence has focus on I (Internal ability) only. Thus, it misses out Effort and analysis of Environmental factors. There is sure shot chance of losing. Then, after losing there comes another E factor – EXCUSE.*

### FOOD FOR THOUGHT

Inaction breeds doubt and fear. Action breeds confidence and courage. If you want to conquer fear, do not sit home and think about it. Go out and get busy.

–Dale Carnegie

# PERFECTION IS MERE PERCEPTION

 r. Singhal is a perfectionist. He keeps on shouting even a paper went missing from its place. He cribs too much as he is not satisfied with others' performance. Everyone associated with him was frustrated and he started losing on relationships. He himself had to over-exert as he was never satisfied with what he was doing. Many of his friends, who used to lend him a helping hand, too stopped taking the risk. As he was ageing, anxiety started taking its toll on him. Very frequently he started getting panic attacks.

## IN A NUTSHELL

1. 'Perfectionist attitude' may give rise to anxiety. When permission is given to self, to make mistakes, chances of errors reduce.
2. Each one works differently. Hence the style is different. A perfectionist can easily damage relationships with his/her compulsive desire for perfection..

## FOOD FOR THOUGHT

A man could do nothing if he waited until he could do it so well that no one could find fault.

–John Henry Newman

# *Instruction not Yet Complete*

was conducting a workshop in a company. Everything was set. Behind the projector screen there was a white board. I had to use the white board but could not find any switch to lift the screen. The co-ordinator said, "Ma'am, pull the screen and leave it…." And I left it accordingly. "Khat….khat….Khat" Few things hit at different sides of the walls. What happened? I was shocked and scared to find that the whole screen had fallen. The co-ordinator said, "Ma'am one word of the instruction was still left, that is 'slowly'." What? That means I had to pull the screen and leave it …. slowly. God! It took fifteen minutes to re-set the room.

### IN A NUTSHELL

1. Missing even one word can create great damage to communication process.
2. My incomplete listening led to a loud noise of breaking the screen and wasting time. In other situations, incomplete listening may cause loud noise in the form of aggression and spoiled relationships.

### FOOD FOR THOUGHT

*I think that you believe you understand what you think I said, but I'm not sure you realise that what you heard is not what I meant.*

–Robert McCloskey

# JUDGEMENT: ARE YOU EMPOWERED?

couple visited a hot place in India (Gaya) during summer. They enjoyed each other's company and did not feel the impact of heat at the place. Rather the place gave them a feeling of warmth. After their return, their friends asked about the feedback on the location. The feedback was extremely wonderful. Next year, another couple visited the same place for some business purpose. But they could not bear the heat. Their feedback about the place was extremely negative.

### IN A NUTSHELL

1. When we are internally positive, the external difficulties do not hit us. The first couple was enjoying each other's company. So, the heat was not bothering them.
2. No heat is more powerful than our mental strength. So, use your mental strength to beat all heat from the environment.

### FOOD FOR THOUGHT

Two men look out the same prison bars; one sees mud and other stars.

–Fredrick Langbridge

## *Intellectual* **EGO**

hen the CCE (Continuous and Comprehensive Education) was implemented by CBSE, teachers had to record data. A few teachers complained, "Are we clerks? Now we need to do so much of writing work?" But complaining did not help them to get rid of the work. They kept spreading the complaining virus. On the other hand, there were groups of teachers who accepted the change and started their job of maintaining records seriously to avoid panic at the last moment. They were enjoying their work.

### IN A NUTSHELL

1. *To be successful in the present world, we need to shed our intellectual ego. "I am a teacher, how can I do typing or writing or taking Photostats" is the sign of intellectual ego. People who remain in the zone of intellectual ego will always remain dissatisfied with their job as they feel that they are being exploited.*
2. *People who can change their mindset along with the changing demands from the situation are the people who quickly reach the top ladder of success and satisfaction.*

### FOOD FOR THOUGHT

*Ego has a voracious appetite, the more you feed it, the hungrier it gets.*

–Nathaniel Bronner Jr.

# WAITING FOR WINNING

It is my habit to reach a place at least half an hour early before the scheduled time. And there is also a vested interest behind it. I complete my writings during 'waiting time.' Once I reached a company half an hour early and found that it was closed. I called the co-ordinator and he was very embarrassed that I had to wait. I told him to take his own time. He hurried and reached the place in 20 minutes. By then, I had completed three pages of my writing. I was satisfied. But the expression on his face made me feel uncomfortable. He was apologising for keeping me waiting. I said politely, "Actually I wish to thank you for providing me the opportunity to write during this waiting time." He was somehow relaxed but his facial expression bore some surprise for me. I did not try to read his mind as I had to focus on the workshop. Next day, he came before time and said, "Participants are yet to come, but you can utilise your waiting time. I too have brought my 'work bag' for use during the waiting time. It was a great learning for me."

## IN A NUTSHELL

1. World is rich in 'waiting time'. A person who can make the best out of it can be the richest in its truest sense.
2. The person using 'waiting time' in fact blesses those people who make him wait. There is no negative feeling involved.
3. You can be an agent of positive behaviour through your own example rather than lecturing.

## FOOD FOR THOUGHT

*A single day is enough to make us a little larger.*

—Paul Klee

## PATTERN OF COMMUNICATION

My son had a magic competition. At that time, I was pre-occupied with my workshops throughout the week. All of a sudden, my instincts as a mother took over a day before the competition and I decided to check his dress. I found that the dress needed some modification. It was 9.00 p.m. Hoping to find the tailoring shop open, I went to the tailor. My son was relieved to see that the shop was still open. So was I. He went to the tailor and said, "Uncle, thank you." The shopkeeper looked at him with surprise. Probably he was the first customer saying thanks before the work. My son was able to sense the curiosity of the tailor. He explained, "Uncle I am saying 'thanks' as you have kept the shop open till now." We shared our problem and he agreed to help us. Soon a boy came and asked in a harsh tone, "Yes, where is my trouser? Have you stitched it?" The tailor said, "No. It would take some time." The boy again replied with rudeness in his voice, "O.K., then give back my trouser." And the tailor returned the same. I said, "Why are you losing a customer?" He said, "You saw how he spoke. Did I say 'no' to you? You see your son came and spoke so politely and how did he speak!"

### IN A NUTSHELL

1. Politeness leads to desired result.
2. In regular life also, we need to make every transaction an energetic and positive experience, whether we get the work done or not. The result would always be satisfying.

### FOOD FOR THOUGHT

*True politeness consists in being easy one's self, and in making every one about one as easy as one can.*

–Alexander Popeh

## POWER OF THOUGHT

here was a recitation competition on the *Hindi Diwas*. I thought I too would give a try. I had come first in the previous year too. My friend, Gagan also took part in the competition. I was touched by her poem. After the competition was over and the result was to be announced, I said, "I think either you would come first or I would come first." The result came. Her name was in the consolation category. I was upset although I was declared first. The result was not yet put up on notice-board. I came home and kept thinking as to why she did not get the first or second prize. Next day, to my surprise a colleague came and congratulated both of us. She broke the news that my friend has come second. I was speechless.

### IN A NUTSHELL

1. The taste of joy on being other's success is boundless.

### FOOD FOR THOUGHT

Caring about others, running the risk of feeling, and leaving an impact on people, brings happiness.

–Harold Kushner

# SMS – Short Message Service or Shattered Mental Stability

ipul was working in a company. One day, he was late to the office. His boss sent him a message: "Where are you?" Vipul sent him a message in reply, which said, "Went for a party yesterday. So, I overslept." His boss became very angry. Vipul was relaxed and was expecting appreciation for his honesty. But the boss was expecting a call from him. When Vipul reached office, he found that his boss was not in a good mood. He was not even talking to him. Vipul sat with his boss and said, "I know you are upset. I really was not able to get up in the morning. But don't worry. I have taken care of the task and it would be over in an hour." There was genuineness and concern in Vipul's voice. Moreover, the facial expression and body language also reflected his genuineness. Task was done in an hour. Boss was relaxed and so was Vipul.

### IN A NUTSHELL

1. In a conflicting situation it is better to have face to face communication to avoid any misunderstanding. In SMS, the reader may miss out some important expression and tone of the sender. He/She may interpret it according to his/her perception.
2. He could have written, "I am sorry to inform that I would be late. I shall share the reason when I meet you."

### FOOD FOR THOUGHT

*If there is any great secret of success in life, it lies in the ability to put yourself in the other person's place and to see things from his point of view – as well as your own.*

–Henry Ford

## TOO MUCH OF EVERYTHING IS BAD

relative of mine was very fond of *gulab jamun*. Out of all sweets, she only loved *gulab jamun*. In the marriage party of her elder sister, she took one *gulab jamun*. Then, the father-in-law of her sister came and requested her to take one more gulab jamun knowing it is her only favourite sweet. She politely said 'no'. Then, her sister's brother-in-law came and requested her to take some more sweets. She was not able to say 'no' to him too. Now, her sister's mother-in-law requested her to take one more *gulab jamun*. She was still not able to say 'no'. She took one more *gulab jamun*. She took all the *gulab jamuns*. But, since then the *gulab jamun* was erased from her 'favourite sweet' list. She satisfied all but spoiled her own taste due to her inability to say 'no'.

### IN A NUTSHELL

1. Too much of everything is bad. Even the 'favourite' can become 'most hated element' if there is too much of it.
2. The four gulab jamuns eaten at certain intervals would not have created a feeling of distaste towards it. This can be applied in relationships too. The favourite of our relationship becomes most hated if we do not give it enough space.

### FOOD FOR THOUGHT

*Love is space and time measured by the heart.*

—Marcel Proust

## LET THEM GET A FEEL

went for a workshop where most of the participants were at their workstations. They seemed to be under lot of work-pressure. More than work pressure, it was 'mental pressure' from the proposed visit of their senior to the office just two days after the workshop. The co-ordinator said, "Ma'am can we start in half-an-hour?" I felt if the programme started in half an hour, it would be difficult to finish what was required for the day." I said, "Please tell them to come and I would give them a break to go back to their workstation. Moreover, if they wish I can also finish the workshop by 3.00 p.m." I just wanted them to get a feel of the workshop. I was sure they would be interested after getting a feel of it. The co-ordinator said, "But they would crib." I was again firm and said, "Let them crib and come. I shall handle the cribbing." I was able to understand the pain of the participants who were not able to come out of their mental pressure. Some amount of push was needed. Then the workshop started. At 2.00 p.m., I said, "Since I promised you to leave by 3.00 p.m., we would be missing a very important topic of 'how to handle losses'." They were all tuned in to the flow of the workshop. They started requesting me to complete everything planned for the day. They did not want to miss a single topic. Prior to starting the workshop, they wanted to compress the 'two-day workshop' into 'one day'. But at the end of the first day, they themselves were saying that they do not want to miss out on the second day session. So, the workshop went on successfully and helped them to ease both mental and work realted pressures. All of them were unanimous that this was the best time to hold such a workshop as they were too pressurised and was feeling incapable of managing the pressure.

### IN A NUTSHELL

1. Some amount of push is needed to make others come out of comfort zone.
2. If there is quality in what you say, you need not force others to listen. They would love to listen to you.

### FOOD FOR THOUGHT

*Comfort zones are more often expanded through discomfort.*
—Peter McWilliams

## MAKE OVER OR TAKE OVER

was going to watch the movie '*Rajneeti*'. We were waiting outside. We had heard so much about the movie that it was difficult for all of us to wait. I thought of watching the surroundings to spend the time and probably getting something to learn too. My eyes fell on the T.V. which was showing an advertisement of Star Plus. I found the logo of Star Plus had changed. I knew that there were many companies who took over other companies. Thus, this must be the case with Star Plus too. I asked my brother, "Has Star Plus been taken over by some other channel?" He said, "No, there has been makeover of their logo." I did not know the reality, but my brother's answer gave me a very important learning.

### IN A NUTSHELL

1. If we '*make over*', keep on creating something new, we will feel new and fresh. Others would also feel the difference.
2. If we don't make over (upgrade skills, talents), we would be taken over.

### FOOD FOR THOUGHT

*They always say time changes things, but you actually have to change them yourself.*

–Andy Warhol

## SERVICE WINS OVER KNOWLEDGE

A teacher was working in a school for long years teaching the senior students but getting only primary grades. Then a vacany arose for a senior teacher's position. She applied, after taking permission from the principal. Though she was prepared, somehow she felt nervous and unsure . Her internal voice said, "I have not been promoted for so many years. I feel this time also I would not be promoted." Anyway, she proceeded for the interview. Just after two persons, it was her chance. The principal came out and said, "Listen, I want to talk to you." The teacher politely went towards the principal. The principal continued, "Today you need not appear for the interview. I shall see your case in July. I am not feeling confident with one of the interviewers. Will you be upset?" The teacher replied, "Ma'am, you asked me to apply for the post and now you are saying me not to appear for the interview. I respect you ma'am and will accept whatever you suggest." The principal thought for a while. She said, "OK, since you have come, can you help us in serving tea?" The teacher enthusiastically replied, "Why not?" And she wholeheartedly tried to manage her emotions and started serving tea. It was almost 4.30 p.m. She was still at the school with two other teachers. Interviews were about to get over. She was waiting at the reception for the instruction on the next tea arrangement. All of a sudden, the supervisor of the school came out and said, "Ma'am wants to talk to you." She was curious to know the reason. Immediately, the principal of the school also came out and told the teacher, "The experts are not happy with any of the candidates. Are you prepared?" The teacher was confused whether to say yes or no. She nodded her head, indicating 'yes'. And she went for the interview. The chairman who was heading the interview board said, "I saw you doing something inside the kitchen with some of your colleagues. What were you doing?" She said, "Sir, it is our duty to serve our elders. I was honoured by this duty given to me. So I was making arrangement for tea and snacks to serve all of you. " All of them felt very satisfied with her answer. They did not ask any subject-based questions as they knew her as a teacher of the senior classes since the last 8 years. Finally, she was selected.

### IN A NUTSHELL

1. The teacher feared that she may not be selected. She was feeding herself with this negative talk. Her initial negative feeding of fear gave her initial trouble.
2. She was upset as she was not allowed to give the interview. But she was genuinely serving her guests. She was doing her duty wholeheartedly. Her service won over.
3. Service is always more important than knowledge.

### FOOD FOR THOUGHT

A merchant who approaches business with the idea of serving the public well has nothing to fear from the competition.
—James Cash Penney

## CHANGE OF FOCUS

Shunali is a very good friend of mine. A few years ago, she lost her only daughter who was six-year old to cancer that was detected only at the last stage. Shunali was shattered. Her life lost all meaning. Nothing could stop her tears. Months passed in the same way. She used to talk to me. One day, I told her, "Why don't you search for a job?" I knew that monetarily she doesn't need a job, but she needs it to get preoccupied with something. I wanted her mind to get into something which needs concentration. She said, "But I am out of touch with the job environment since last 8 years." I advised her to surf the internet and update herself with new skills. She joined a computer course and simultaneously prepared her resume. She also started looking for job opportunities. Within 15 days, her depression reduced. She was not only able to manage her regular work on schedule but also kept her emotions under control. There were moments when she would sink in sorrow and tears roll down, but the frequency of attack came down. She is now working for differentially-abled children and found a new meaning for her living.

### IN A NUTSHELL

1. Just as physical injury takes time to heal, emotional injury also takes time to heal. So, have patience and give some time for emotional healing.
2. As soon as we change our focus into something away from the aspect of diffi culty, even the diffi cult situation becomes easier to handle.
3. The more we keep talking about diffi culty, the more our thoughts become paralysed. Thus, forcing oneself to think constructively and getting into a constructive work pattern is important to escape from the diffi cult situation.

### FOOD FOR THOUGHT

You and I are not what we eat; we are what we think.
—Walter Anderson

## ACTIVE Vs EFFECTIVE

was one of the panel members for selection of head boy/ head girl in DAV, Sreshtha Vihar, Delhi. Our plan was to select students from class XII. But one student who was the council member in class XI, also appeared for the interview. When asked what he did as a council member, he replied, "I was active throughout." When he was asked to specify any particular activity which he found most effective during his tenure as a council member, he was not able to specify. He was active but not effective.

### IN A NUTSHELL

1. It doesn't matter how active we are until and unless we are effective.
2. At the end of the day, one needs to review whether his activeness brought any amount of effectiveness.
3. 'How effective I was' analysis is essential for success.

### FOOD FOR THOUGHT

*Action to be effective must be directed to clearly conceived ends.*
—Jawaharlal Nehru

## *Famous Vs Popular*

went for a workshop in a company. In that group, a member made a belated entry. There was heavy applause. When I asked for the reason, the participants said that he was very popular for his quarrelsome nature. Then came the occasion in the workshop where everyone had to appreciate each other. One participant was praised for his service towards birds. Since the last 21 years, he had been doing the same in addition to his routine office work. Strangely, no one appreciated the quarrelsome participant.

### IN A NUTSHELL

1. It is useless to be popular and being disliked by all.
2. When a person does something for others on a consistent basis without any selfish motive, he becomes famous. But a person hungry for fame can never be famous.
3. Becoming famous is a gradual process. In between, one has to swallow many pains.
4. Mother Teresa never served society to be famous. She did as she felt the pain of others. Relieving pain of others gave her the real reward. In that process, she also became famous.

### FOOD FOR THOUGHT

*Avoid popularity if you would have peace.*

–Abraham Lincoln

# Cut

went to a 'paper box' making factory where ladies made packets and boxes of paper. Some ladies were cutting the paper at a particular place and passing on to the next group of ladies for folding it. One lady from another group was seen keeping one cut paper to the side. I asked why she kept the paper at the side. She replied, "The cut was not at the right place."

## IN A NUTSHELL

1. To achieve success, we need to cut certain unnecessary things. For example, if we watch too much of TV and we don't cut it, we would be simply wasting our precious time.
2. In our relationships too we need to know what and when to cut. Generally, in the race for success in career we often cut family relationships and that will become self-damaging. It is very difficult to repair the cuts in a relation. The 'sorry' glue rarely helps to heal the inner bleeding.

## FOOD FOR THOUGHT

*Hot heads and cold hearts never solved anything.*

–Billy Graham

# Old is Gold

It was the annual function of a school. My friend's son was participating in one programme. At night, her son said that madam had asked him to wear blue jeans. My friend was annoyed that he did not give the information on time. It was already 10.30 p.m. Suddenly, she remembered that she had kept some old clothes for donating to the poor. She opened her 'pitara' (bag) and took out an old jeans. Her son too became happy as he could participate in the programme as instructed by the teacher.

## IN A NUTSHELL

1. The old jeans appeared to be new after it was kept away for a certain period. Thus, if a relation appears to be stressful, take a mental distance and come back again with renewed freshness.
2. Just as the old jeans was needed at a moment of crisis, any old relationship can also be of great use. So, we should never throw a relation. If we feel too much strained with any relation, we can just leave it for sometime on a positive note and come back to feel the beauty of the relation.

## FOOD FOR THOUGHT

A real friend is one who walks in when the rest of the world walks out.

—Walter Winchell

## POWER OF SELF-CONTROL

here was a programme organised by a religious organisation, which my son and I attended. My son saw an elephant that was part of the religious procession and he wanted to take a ride on it. My friend Komal asked about the charges for it. The Mahout said that he would take Rs.50/-. I always want to teach Hemang (my son) the value of money. I looked at him to see his response. He immediately said, "Mamma, it is too much. Let me not ride." I felt like giving him Rs. 50/- for a ride. But I controlled myself. I did not want to destroy his understanding and self-control. I told myself that at some other time I would fulfill his wish. After half an hour through the procession, my son started walking by the side of the elephant. One gentleman, who was part of that religious organisation saw him and asked the Mahout to take him to the elephant's top. Already there were three children, so the Mahout was reluctant. But the gentleman insisted that there was space for at least four children. So, the Mahout had to take Hemang also. He was very happy. So were I and my friend Komal.

### IN A NUTSHELL

1. My son tried to control what he wanted. Sometimes, in life, when we control our short term desires, we get long term benefit.
2. When we wish for something very passionately, we will get it. My son wanted to be with the elephant. As he did not get the opportunity to sit on the elephant, he was enjoying its company by walking beside it. His happiness to be at the side of the elephant brought the additional happiness of being on the back of the elephant. Similarly, when we want something passionately and if we don't get it initially, we should not stop worrying. Rather the joy we create within us would get transferred to real life accomplishment of our object of passion. This is the law of attraction that works universally.

### FOOD FOR THOUGHT

*To wish you were is to waste the person you are.*

# NATURAL LEARNING

was driving with my son at the back seat. He was lying. I wanted to talk to him. He said that he wanted to lie down for 10 minutes. I did not say anything. I recalled the day when I started driving a few years ago. At that time my son was talking to me. I said, "Dear, you are seeing that Mamma is driving. Talk to me after we get down." What a difference! He wanted to talk to me yesterday and I was busy in driving. Today, I want to talk to him and he wants to lie down. I thought to myself whatever I do; I need to share time with my son at any cost. Since then, whenever he had to share his emotions or feelings, I made it a point to lend an attentive ear instantly. And it worked to strengthen our bond.

## IN A NUTSHELL

*Many a time we ignore the relations that are very close to us. We take them for granted saying that 'we are busy'. But this statement 'we are busy' crushes the emotional bond with the other person who has intense desire to talk or be with us. Then a stage comes when we wish to go near them when they have gone far away from us.*

## FOOD FOR THOUGHT

*I have feelings too. I am still human. All I want is to be loved, for myself and my talent.*

–Marilyn Monroe

## QUALIFIED BUT UNQUALIFIED TO BE EMPLOYED

helpless mother came to me for counselling. Her son was hyperactive and was having learning disability. I thought we need to work in collaboration with teachers, parents and peers to help the child. In that process, I went to the class teacher. I just mentioned the child's name and she showered all the aggression of the child on me. She also called a few children to testify that she was right. I forcibly sent the children back and tried to explain the problem, but she was busy sharing her own pain. I found that interacting with her was of no use at all. So, I started taking the help of the child's peer group. They beautifully and sincerely helped the child. They also tried to change the mindset of the teacher.

### IN A NUTSHELL

1. *Every teacher needs a professional degree of B.Ed. to get entry into any good school as a teacher. But after they get employment, they become unqualified for the job. Is that teacher a good person who criticises the child rather than making efforts to give a joyful childhood? Is the person a teacher who gossips in the staffroom? Is that person a teacher who de-motivates a parent in parent-teacher meeting? It is very essential to provide continuous training to keep this kind of teacher really qualified.*
2. *Where adult mind remains blocked, we can also take help of children's mind. They can be of great help.*

### FOOD FOR THOUGHT

*They may forget what you said, but they will never forget how you made them feel.*

–Carl W. Buechner

# *Two people – One situation – Two responses*

Two ladies, Mrs. Sheetal and Mrs. Chaitali who were working in the same company were expecting promotion. There were other candidates too. Both of them did not get the promotion and were disappointed. Mrs. Sheetal went for a trip to Shimla which was fixed earlier. Mrs. Chaitali cancelled her trip as she was not in a mood to enjoy. Mrs. Sheetal came back after a week. She started taking care of her work. But Mrs. Chaitali was in her same 'pain zone'. One day Mrs. Chaitali told Mrs. Sheetal, "Management insulted us by not giving the promotion which we deserved. So, I have stopped working and you too should do the same." Mrs. Sheetal replied, "I am feeling better as I have started working. Rather than taking revenge and giving myself pain, I wish to live in peace. Moreover, do you feel not working would give you promotion? It would only bring depression in you." Mrs. Chaitali thought that Mrs. Sheetal was foolish. Days passed. Mrs. Chaitali had to work as there was risk in her job. But she fell victim to a stomach disease. Doctors described her problem as psycho-somatic. She ended up spending a lot of money in consulting psychologists for a cure.

## IN A NUTSHELL

1. Changing focus gives great emotional healing power. Mrs. Sheetal went to Shimla after the company refused to give her permotion. Although she was feeling low, going to Shimla helped her to come out of her low feeling. Changing focus can be done by spending time with someone we love the most, spending time with something we enjoy the most.
2. When we are taking revenge we are not hurting others but actually hurting ourselves. Revenge is a deadly trap which keeps us in the stinking drain of sorrow. Moving forward and creating the best out of what we have is the best constructive revenge.

### FOOD FOR THOUGHT

*Ever more people today have the means to live, but no meaning to live for.*

—Victor E. Frankl

## How Actual is 'Actually'

have a wonderful friend named Vibha. These days she is slightly getting fatter. I asked her, "Why don't you exercise?" Without thinking she responded, "Actually I don't have time." I thought for a while and said, "Do you think that I have no work?" We counted and it was found that I had more assignments than her. Despite that I do exercise. I tried to convince her. But still her 'actually' stopped her from being convinced. Till date she has not commenced exercising. She started having problem in the joints also. But she prefers to take medicine than exercising regularly. Each one of us is acquainted with this word 'actually'. A person comes late and tells, "Actually there was lot of traffi c"; a person commits a mistake and tells, "Actually I was thinking something else"; a person who fails in achieving tells, "Actually my parents were not educated". There are many people who are victims of 'actually' and doing nothing meaningful in life.

### IN A NUTSHELL

1. Until and unless we come out of the 'actually' zone, we cannot do the actual things of life.
2. We need to know that 'actually' is actually blocking our road to success. So, we actually need to break it as soon as possible and then, move ahead towards the actual growth.

### FOOD FOR THOUGHT

*People with integrity do what they say they are going to do. Others have excuses.*

—Laura Schlessinger

## *Reject Better than React*

It was morning time. My son was having breakfast and I was having my morning tea sitting close to him. He was talking to me. We both were in a good mood. I was teasing him to see how he handles the situation. He was just smiling. I asked, "I am teasing you and you are not saying anything!" He said, "By not saying anything, I am rejecting your teasing." I felt great and proud as a mother that he knows how to handle such situations and maintain his self-esteem.

### IN A NUTSHELL

1. *It is better to reject rather than to react. Rejecting would create full stop to the argument but would carry on the relationship. Reacting would create full stop to the relationship and carry on the argument.*
2. *Even a child can be a good 'situation and relationship manager'. So, open the door of learning for any channel.*

### FOOD FOR THOUGHT

The possibilities are numerous once we decide to act and not react.

–Charles R. Swindoll

## LOSS OF MOBILE OR LOSS OF SELF-ESTEEM

uresh, who was working in a well-known company, lost his mobile phone. It was just loss of a mobile phone. When I asked him, "How many days did it take you to come out of the sense of loss?" He said, "It took some five to six days." I asked, "I can't believe. You seem so composed and thoughtful. A mobile loss took you six days to heal?" He explained, "Actually I had the conviction that I don't lose anything. I can take good care of all things. But the loss of the mobile was a big shock to my belief system."

### IN A NUTSHELL

1. Everyone has faced some or other kind of loss. But how one comes out of the loss depends on various factors. Like for Suresh, it was more of losing his self-esteem than the mobile.
2. As loss and gains are part of life we need to cope with it effectively so that we don't lose much of our emotional energy.

### FOOD FOR THOUGHT

Low self-esteem is like driving through life with your hand-brake on.

## COMPETITION VS ENVY

here was a person in an organisation who wanted to compete against his colleagues. He was crazy to get promotion and was struggling hard to get it. The time for appraisal came and he succeeded in getting the promotion. But after coming home, he felt unhappy again. When asked about the reason, he said, "I am unhappy because after coming home I learnt that my neighbour bought a Mercedes."

### IN A NUTSHELL

1. Competition says, "I want to win." Envy says, "Whether I win or not, he/she should not win."
2. Competition = Desire to win + Effort
   Envy= Desire to inject pain to others + Nasty effort towards desire

### FOOD FOR THOUGHT

*Envy shoots at others and wounds itself.*

## DISCOMFORT LEADS TO SATISFACTION

went to Agra with my son. It was scorching heat. When we reached there, we found that we had to go barefoot up till the Taj Mahal entrance. As soon as we opened our shoes and the feet touched the heated floor, we started running as if being chased by a cheetah. Within two minutes, we reached the entrance that was a shaded place. It was a great relief. I thought, it was only because of the feeling of discomfort that we reached the entrance within two minutes.

### IN A NUTSHELL

1. The discomfort in our situation was burning feet, and the vision was reaching the Taj Mahal. As we reached there, it gave a feeling of satisfaction. Thus, when we are dissatisfied, we need to search for vision.
2. Our focus was to see the Taj Mahal. But with the discomfort our focus changed. We were more interested to save our feet first. Thus, discomfort changes our focus. So, we may distract from our actual goal. Thus, while searching for comfort, we need to ask ourselves that are we moving in the direction of our actual goal or just saving ourselves from discomfort.

### FOOD FOR THOUGHT

*Discomfort is very much part of my master plan.*
—Jonathan Lethem

## STRETCHING THE KNOWLEDGE ZONE

was sitting with some of my colleagues. Ms Meenakshi was sharing one of her life's incidents with me. When she was around 14 years old, her father asked her to send a letter through registry. She was nervous as for the first time she was going to the post office alone. She gathered her courage and went to the post office. She recalled what her father said, "Give the letter to the post master and after weighing he would mention the cost of the stamps the letter would require." She did the same. Rs. 15 was the required amount for the stamp. She affixed the stamps and dropped in the letter box. With lot of pride, she came back. Father asked, "Where is the receipt?" She was surprised, "Which receipt?" Father replied, "The receipt which the post master must have given you after the registry was done." She surprisingly said, "But I dropped the letter in the letter box!" Father was shocked and slightly angry now, "Then, what was the need to weigh the letter and stick stamp of Rs. 15?" Little Meenakshi thought for a while and said, "OK Papa, let me go again." She went to the post office, contacted the post master, explained her mistake, made a humble request to open the letter box and help her. The post master was able to sense her genuineness and opened the letter box. It took approximately 10 minutes to take out the right letter. But this was second time that Ms Meenakshi came back home with an extra sense of pride.

### IN A NUTSHELL

1. *Giving incomplete instruction can be harmful. Moreover, feedback needs to be taken whether the other person has grasped the required instruction in the right manner.*
2. *It is OK to commit mistake, but it is important to develop courage to mend the mistake.*

### FOOD FOR THOUGHT

*Champions keep playing until they get it right.*

–Billie Jean King

**THE BEST OF SELF HELP BOOKS**

## How to Become a Successful Speaker & Presenter

Format: Paperback
Language: English
Pages: 112
Price: ₹ 108.00

*Have you ever thought of addressing an audience and making them listen to you without batting an eyelid? Do you want to create a trance-like spell on people listening to your speech?*

The book *How to become a Successful Speaker & Presenter* will let you do that. It has carefully dissected every aspect of public speaking and presents a clear map that any aspiring speaker can follow. Besides, it also incorporates the necessary techniques to motivate, captivate, and persuade the audience while making various presentations, etc.

You will master 'How to'
- Conquer stage fright
- Organize material in a flowing manner
- Customise speech for different sets of gathering
- Inspire audience
- Include humour and maintain eye contact
- Involve people interactively
- Maintain friendly yet professional image, tone and diction
- Invite queries
- Thank the audience for paying attention to your speech

This book contains preparation material for beginners, as well as for experienced. This book is a must-read for students, executives, managers, and others who wish to improve their oratory skills.

*How to become a Successful Speaker & Presenter* has been carefully thought out to make an easy and interesting read to leave you buzzing with ideas on how you can implement the ideas and plans for speaking effectively in public.

**The Best of Self Help Books**

## SUCCESS THROUGH POSITIVE THINKING

Format: Paperback • Language: English
Pages: 176 • Price: ₹ 96.00

The author of this book, S.P. Sharma, not only discusses the problems faced by modern man in this book, but also explains certain religious truths in a comprehensive manner in non-technical language.
It contains useful information designed to help one relieve from anxiety and disturbing thoughts – providing a clear vision leading to a happier life.
It would help one:
- Combat the shocks of life
- Know that nothing is more useful than the awakened self
- Understand the principles that make life happier

It is a wonderful work for anyone who desires to get Success Through Positive Thinking.

## Youngster's Guide for PERSONALITY DEVELOPMENT

Format: Paperback • Language: English
Pages: 120 • Price: ₹ 88.00

In a world marked by competition, personality is the key to success – whether it is social or business or personal or political arena. Interview for IAS or an MNC, meeting with the parents of your prospective bride, addressing a public rally, or delivering a speech in an international conference...if you have a confident and pleasing personality, you will surely make your mark! This book seeks to motivate young men and women, particularly students, to make conscious and continuous effort to build character and develop good personality.

## Books on Mind & Body

### BODY Language

Format: Paperback • Language: English • Pages: 120 • Price: ₹ 108.00

Communication is not always through sound or language. Much can be said with gestures or movement of eyes. In fact, more often than not, the Body Language says more than words.

Now discover all the finer points and nuances of body language in this masterly work:
- How thumb gesture displays dominance, superiority and aggression
- How dilation of eyes sends romantic signal
- How a sideways glance indicates either hostility or interest

### PEACE of MIND

Format: Paperback • Language: English• Pages: 174 • Price: ₹ 96.00

Peace of mind does not just mean soothing your mind. It also does not mean escaping into a dream world. It means your most effective involvement in a real world.

In fact, Peace of mind greatly increases our intellectual power and enables us to think rationally and in a better way.

Hari Dutt Sharma has written this book in a unique poetic style that could be termed as Elated Prose which makes it most interesting for the reader. It tells you how peace of mind can be attained through fighting the negative emotions like anger, jealousy, hatred and greed, etc. Compounded with its simplicity and down-to-earth approach, it leads you to discover the enemies of peace and thus attain inner peace.

**Books for Career Management**

## CHANAKYA
Rules of Governance by the Guru of Governance

Format: Paperback
Language: English
Pages: 248
Price: ₹ 175.00

Chanakya was both a destructive and creative thinker able to annihilate an established empire and erect and establish another larger, richer and greater on the debris, without money, material and man. So, he is the only qualified person in human history to be Guru; Acharya; Teacher; Guide and Mentor in the field of Management. With his super mind and supreme determination he succeeded in everything and everywhere; and wrote down everything without inhibitions or secrecy for the posterity in his three monumental works: Chanakya Niti; Chanakya Suttra and Kautilya Arthashastra. Read this book Chanakya: Rules of Governance by the Guru of Governance for all the details of his life; legendary books, and secrets of success in any or every field of Management.

1. Teachings of Kautilya's Arthashastra & Nitishastra
2. Perfect Analogy between Ancient Managerial System & Modern Corporate Setup
3. Practical Knowledge from Chanakya's Maxims on Life & Living

*BOOKS FOR CAREER MANAGEMENT*

## BUSINESS
### QUIZ BOOK

Format: Paperback
Language: English
Pages: 256
Price: ₹ 200.00

Did you know that crossword puzzles first appeared in the New York World in 1913, and soon became a popular feature in newspapers or that Kellog's as a brand had spent more than 100 years, $4000 on one page ad in the July issue of the Ladies Home Journal, Apple had lured John Sculley away from Pepsi because they wanted him to apply his marketing skills to the personal computer market. Find facts and trivia from the world of business that will amaze and delight you. The questions in this book have been framed in a way that they are: guessable with intelligent, lateral, or lucky thinking; interesting, amusing, or surprising; enjoyable, even to people who think they don't like quizzes; not so difficult that nobody knows the answer.

There are over 30 sections from automobiles, advertising, businessmen, FMCG to publications, management terms, quality control, management quotes. A special section for visual questions that are part of almost every business quiz these days has also been included.

The book will serve not just as a stepping stone for people who are interested in business quizzing but will prove to be an ideal compendium for all aspirants aiming for admission to professional colleges or career options in banking, insurance, defence, railways, state & central government services, besides many other top tier professions.

## Books for Career Management

### 10 FUNDAMENTAL RULES OF SUCCESS

Format: Paperback • Language: English • Pages: 124 • Price: ₹ 96.00

The purpose of this book is to share with the readers the 10 fundamental rules to achieve success compiled from the vast ocean of literature on success. Some of these essential rules include – setting a goal, positive attitude and self confidence, purposeful desire, planning and preparation, resources, inputs, discipline, action, persistence or perseverance, prayer and values.

Here success is first defined; then the basic rules involved in achieving success are enumerated and explained with relevant anecdotes and stories. Besides these 10 fundamental rules, a set of success formulae as well as virtue capsules have also been added in the book.

### PREPARING for a Winning INTERVIEW

Format: Paperback • Language: English • Pages: 233 • Price: ₹ 150.00

The book *'Preparing for a Winning Interview'* is divided into two sections. The first section deals with the preparations, research and understanding various facts of the interview and its procedure.

The second section contains understanding and learning specific job skills in ever-changing and challenging corporate environment; the role of an employee and the need to be prepared beforehand to fit in different organisation by meeting tough corporate tasks, and by coping with the changing works, conditions and milieu

www.ingramcontent.com/pod-product-compliance
Lightning Source LLC
Chambersburg PA
CBHW070337230426
43663CB00011B/2349